BERLIN
ARTS GUIDE

IRENE BLUMENFELD

GW00706001

ART GUIDE PUBLICATIONS

Art Guide Publications.

Paris Art Guide   Fiona Dunlop   ISBN 0 9507160 65
London Art & Artists Guide   Heather Waddell   ISBN 0 946716 50 1
New York Art Guide   Deborah Jane Gardener   ISBN 0 9507160 9X
Australian Arts Guide   Roslyn Kean   ISBN 0 9507160 81
Berlin Arts Guide   Irene Blumenfeld   ISBN 0 946716 40 4
Amsterdam Art Guide   Christian Reinewald   ISBN 0 946716 35 8
The Artist's Directory   H. Waddell/R. Layzell   ISBN 0 946716 005

British Library Cataloguing in Publication Data
Berlin Arts Guide.
1. Art - Berlin — Handbook, manuals etc.,
2. Berlin (Germany) — Handbook, manuals etc.,
1. Blumenfeld, Irene
914.3'15504878 DD859
ISBN 0 946716 40 4

Art Guide series © Art Guide Publications
Text copyright © Irene Blumenfeld
Maps © 1986
Photographs copyright Christiane Hartmann © 1986
Published by Art Guide Publications Ltd., 28 Colville Road,
London W11 2BS. Telephone 01-229 4669
Typeset and printed by AGP Newspapers Ltd.
Telephone 01-870 0769

Cover photo: *Wolf Vostell at the Wewerka Gallery*
                 Christiane Hartmann

CONTENTS

WEST BERLIN

Das Berliner Kunstleben

Berlin gibt es zweimal. Dei Stadt gehört je zu einer Hälfte den beiden ideologischen Giganten an, die sich unsere Welt zur Zeit nach Ost und West hin teilen. Die Museen gibt es alle ebenfalls zweimal. Vom Museum für Vor- und Frühgeschichte bis hin zur National galerie trägt ein Institut im Osten wie im Westen den gleichen Namen.

So etwas wie ein öffentliches Kunstleben gibt es allerdings nur in West-Berlin. Zu Museen, Kunsthallen und bezirksamtlichen Ausstellungsstätten treten an die 180 private Galerien.

Dabei ist Berlin nie vorwiegend eine Stadt der bilbenden Künste gewesen. Berlin ist eine Musik- und Theaterstadt. Erst in den letzten zwanzig Jahren hat sich auch auf dem Gebiet der beldenden Künste eine 'Szene' — von Eingeweihten übrigeus englisch ausgesprochen, 'scene' — entwickelt. Das Interesse an Kunst mub sich sprungartig gesteigert haben, denn um 1960 gab es an die zehn bis 15 Galerien. Bei den Vernissagen kannte jeder jeden.

Das ist längst nicht mehr der Fall. Die Verhältnisse haben sich umgekehrt. Kunst zieht heute mehr Zuschauer an als etwa Fubballspiele. Sie steht im Mittelpunkt des Interesses.

Die Ursachen sind vielschichtig. Das Künstler progamme des Deutschen Akademischen Austauschdiente (DAAD) hat Jahr für Jahr prominente und Nachwuchs-Künstler aus dem Ausland eingeladen. Manche von ihnen (etwa Edward Keinholz oder Peter Sedgley) blieben auf Dauer. Auf jeden Fall haben sie Berlin als Stätte der Künste international bekannt gemacht. Die Tradition der Künstler-Selbsthilfe-Galerien hat ein übriges getan. Aus der Galerie 'Grobgörschen' wuchs ein eigener Stil, der Kritische Realismus, aus der Galerie am Moritzplatz die Schule der 'Neuen Wilden', die sich hier lieber 'Heftige' nennen. Sie, Neo-Expressionisten, die meist bei Karl Horst Hödicke an der hiesigen Hochschule der Künste (HdK) studiert haben, fanden — wie ihre Kollegen der italienischen 'Arte Cifra' — weltweiten Erfolg bis hin zum New Yorker Kunsthandel. Aktive Galeristen, darunter auffallend viele Galeriestinnen, sind hinzugetreten.

Neben der immer noch international bedeutenden Deutschen Oper, dem regen Musikleben, den staatlichen und privaten Bühnen, hat sich gleichberechtigt die 'scene' entfaltet. Wer deutsche Kunst kennenlernen will, die klassiche wie die allerneueste, moderne, bub früher oder später nach Berlin kommen, nach wie vor einer heimlichen Hauptstadt jedenfalls der Künste.

Heinz Ohff.

4

Joseph Beuys at his Berlin exhibition

The Berlin Artlover

There are two Berlins. The city is shared between the two ideological giants that divide our world: East and West. In the same way there are two sets of museums in Berlin. There is for example a Pre-historic museum in the East as well as in the West and there are two National Galleries.

 An open art life however exists only in the west. More than 180 galleries can be added to museums, art institutions and exhibition houses run by the District Offices. Nevertheless Berlin was never a city which primarily concentrated on the Fine Arts. Berlin was always more a city of music and theatre. It has only been during the last twenty years that an art scene — which is pronounced as the English 'scene' by those in the know — has developed. Interest in the Fine Arts must have blossomed suddenly because by 1960 there were 10-15 private galleries and everybody knowseverybody else at private views.

There are many reasons for this. The Artists' Programme of the German Academic Exchange Service (DAAD) has invited annually foreign artists, some already famous, others still 'rising' for a stay in the city. Some even stayed for good (Edward Keinholz or Peter Sedgeley). Berlin gained an international look.

Much has also been done by the Berlin tradition of "Self Help" galleries. Young painters founded the gallery "Grobgoschen" from which a new style was derived that of "Critical Realism". The gallery at the Moritzplatz became the home of the "New Fauves", called in Berlin "Vehements" or "impetuous". The Neo-Expresssionists, mostly former students of Karl Horst Hodicke at the Berlin Art School (HDK), have found international acclaim, like their colleagues from the Italian 'Arte Cifra' even in the New York art world. The active gallerists, among them many lady dealers, complete the picture.

A world famous Opera House, an exciting music life and a lively theatre attract interest in Berlin but there is also an "art scene". Anyone who wants to know about German art, classical or the latest most modern style has to come to Berlin — still the capital of Germany, at least in the field of arts.

BERLIN

Berlin is an unique city pocketed in the middle of East Germany. It is still occupied by four nations' troops — the Soviets in the East and West Berlin is divided into a French, a British and an American Sector. It is indeed a fascinating city one where a whole range of activities are possible.

The division between West and East, since 1961 defined by the wall, divides not only thought and philosophy but culture. The old city centre is now part of East Berlin and with the division many theatres and museums are no longer in the West. The programme has therefore been for West Berlin to re-build a city with among other things a new National Gallery (designed by Mies van der Rohe), a new Philharmonic Hall and new theatres (including the Peter Stein inspired Schaubühne in Lehniner Square). The 'centre' has been transferred to Kurfürstendamm (Ku'Damm) and here it is always crowded with people. Along this street are many shops and in summer it doubles in size as the cafes and restaurants spill out onto the pavement.

It is around the Ku'Damm to the north and south that most of the commercial galleries can be found, centering on such streets as Fasanen and around Savigny Square. They are not however near enough to each other to be seen in a short time and it is worth spending time discovering them and also venturing to the other pockets of galleries, for instance near the Tiergarten and around the National Gallery. Museums are also not to be found in one location and Berlin is certainly a city which gives surprising rewards for a small amount of investigation and a good guidebook.

Due to Berlin's rather unique political situation there has grown up a less established art world in the West. This is largely initiated by the artists themselves, of which there is a huge international community, and it is often in collaboration with and with financial help from Der Senator für Kulturelle Angelegenheiten (The Senator for Cultural Business). These artists' initiatives are wide ranging and have included installations in a stairwell, a bank's safe and an ice stadium not to mention sites such as factories and artist-run galleries. There is also in each of the 11 districts of West Berlin a Kunstamt (Art Office) which, with varying enthusiasm depending on the area, goes a long way to creating a focal point for the local community of the visual and performance arts in the area.

West Berlin is, as many people know, a city of festivals. Apart from regulars such as the annual Film Festival every occasion is seen to be an excuse for a chain of events and happenings. An example of this is the recent Bundesgartenschau (Federal Garden Show) which had a very comprehensive programme of lectures, events and performances. Sculpture was specially commissioned for the main park which was built on an area of wasteland and will continue to be a public park. Organisations such as the Deutscher Akademischer Austauschdienst (DAAD) invite annually visual artists, writers, composers, filmmakers and architects, from different countries, to come and live in Berlin for a year. There is also a regular festival for cultures from other countries called Horizonte. All this activity has attracted a great many different nationalities to discover Berlin and many have stayed.

The new Literaturhaus.

Berlin is certainly a city of contrasts and any tension created by the ever obvious presence of the wall dividing the city is contrasted by the relaxed level of life. Some commercial galleries in West Berlin, for instance, only open in the afternoon and on Saturday morning and some artist-run spaces are open only a few hours a week. The fact that both are well attended shows the seriousness with which the Berliners view art. The East part of Berlin has many contrasts too and is in many ways very Westernized. Much investment for improvement does in fact come from the West to keep the vital routes of transport and communication open. East Berlin is justly proud of its museums and although the National Gallery's modern collection has largely been restored to the West they have the magnificent Pergamon Alter. The old Opera House is also in the East, on the sweeping side street called Under den Linden (Under the Lime Trees). It is possible from the West to go to their performances as well as to the theatre and the Senate for Cultural Business prints a diary of events called 'Kultur' which covers the whole of Berlin.

Returning from the East you might be tempted to go to the other extreme and visit the huge store called KaDeWe (Kaufhaus des Westerns — Store of the West). Where, on the top floor, is the reportedly largest food department in the world. From the entrance of KaDeWe one can see a reminder of the destruction of the city during the 2nd World War in the form of the Kaiser Wilhelm Church. This was left damaged and a new annexe has been built, in the modern style. West Berlin has however, above all, belief in the future and it is perhaps most clearly seen through it's re-building strategy. Development of the city is planned with the publicly expressed hope that Berlin will once again by a re-united city.

Joanna Littlejohns.

Graffiti on the Wall at Kreuzberg

BERLIN — Impressions of a City

Living in Berlin, one of the things that you are never allowed to forget is that it is a walled city. Roads which once led somewhere don't anymore. Instead you are confronted with a 3 meter high 'running fence' this time however several meters thick, made in concrete and there to stay.

Berlin has witnessed many changes in the last half century and in many ways it has come to terms with 'the wall'. Indeed it has become a tourist attraction — you don't visit Berlin and not see the wall. It appears on the surface anyway to be a relaxed easy going city, but beneath that, there is still a strong element of uncertainty. It is still a 'front line' city always looking back over its shoulder.

Over the years the wall has been daubed with graffiti and political statements, painted by artists trying to disguise its very existence. One artist recently using many gallons of petrol attempted to burn it down, more a political statement than an act of vandalism — but it still stands.

There is a grittiness about Berlin. It is like an old war-horse that refuses to die, and behind its skin deep rather transparent polished facade there is a rawness which is very strong and appealing.

It is because of these qualities that I feel so many artists are attracted to Berlin. Admittedly there is a very healthy support system that fuels the city that is constantly dangling there like a carrot. However this surely can not be the only reason that so many stay.

A large proportion of the artists in Berlin work and live in an area called Kreusberg. It is a bizarre quarter of the city, offering a strange mixture of urban decay and a new found vitality. Populated largely by Turks there is much poverty — but there is also a strength and an energy. It pretends to be nothing else than what it is existing in stark contrast to the more fashionable, more acceptable yet more expensive parts of Berlin, where there are forests and lakes, where you can swim and sail. Indeed Berlin is, as has been stated many times before, a city of contrast, but it is not until you have lived and worked in the city that you understand what that really means.

Eric Snell
DAAD Artist in Berlin

Rainer Fetting, one of Berlin's foremost "New Fauves"

FINE ARTS

STIFTUNG PREUBISCHER KULTURBESITZ
THE PRUSSIAN MUSEUMS COLLECTION

The Prussian Museum collection was begun by Kaiser Friedrich Wilhelm in the late 17th century and enlarged by his successors Friedrich I and II. By 1830 the collection celebrated its public opening in a museum especially designed by the architect Schinkel. 100 years later Berlin boasted 19 state museums established in 15 different buildings. This extraordinary process was interrupted by fascism and war in the 1930's and 40's.

The post-war period has been one of re-housing, re-establishing and continuing the pre-1933 tradition. The collection is now divided into 14 museums, some at Dahlem — mostly displayed there in the superb buildings of 1970 designed by Bruno Paul — some in the restored buildings of and across from the Charlottenburg Palace and some in the continuingly developing Tiergarten cultural centre. Dahlem displays the museums of Ethnography, India, Islam, The Far East, German Folklore, the paintings' gallery 1300-1800, the sculpture collection, the prints and drawings collection and the Junior and Blind Museums. Charlottenburg displays the museums of Greek and Roman Antiquities, Ancient Egypt, pre and proto-history and houses the plaster cast house and the Art Library. Tiergarten can boast the New National Gallery showing 19th and 20th century painting and sculpture, the Musical Instruments' Museum, the Arts and Crafts' Museum and the State Library. Together they create a varied combination of locations and architecture which itself reflects Berlin's history and present.

There is no mustiness about these museums; each is singularly appealing, refined yet welcoming, with clear directions, knowledgeable and friendly staff, worthwhile information sheets about each section and catalogues, books, postcards and posters to buy as memories of a rich experience. The originality, sensitivity and beauty in the means chosen for display are exceptional and add even more to the excitement one feels in seeing centuries of human art.

MUSEUM FÜR VÖLKERKUNDE
Ethnographical Museum
Lansstraße 8, 1000 Berlin 33, Telephone 830 1248. Open Tuesday-Sunday 9-5. Closed Monday.
Underground Dahlem Dorf
Where does one begin? This is one of the world's largest collections of ethnography, displayed with outstanding clarity and artistry. There are five sections, each with its own style: Old America, Africa, the South Seas, Southern Asia, and East Asia. Where does one spend longest, the stone sculpture from Guatemala, the original boats and houses from the South Seas, Tang ceramics, theatre and cult masks or shadow-play figures and dolls from South Asia? It is, perhaps, best not to try and decide but to be simply transported from one section to another (although this would be rather tiring in one day!). Remember the information sheets are a useful guide or a refresher course later. Only one warning — you will be overwhelmed!

GEMÄLDEGALERIE
Paintings' Gallery
Arnimallee 23/27, 1000 Berlin 33, Telephone 8301248
Open Tuesday-Sunday 9-5pm. Closed Monday.
Underground: Dahlem Dorf
A display of some of the finest European paintings from the 12th to the 18th centuries inclusive. The selection of German, Dutch, French, Italian and English painting is one of the world's major collections, exquisitely displayed and really worthy of many visits. The German section concentrating on the Middle Ages and the Renaissance is of course significant; of special note are paintings by Hans Holbein and Albrecht Dürer.

The gallery is divided between two floors, the ground floor including Italian painting from 1300-1600, Old German painting from 1300-1600, Old Netherlands painting from 1500-1600 and German, French and Enlgish painting from 1800-1900, while the upper floor shows Flemish and Dutch Baroque painting and French and Italian Baroque and Rococo painting. Caravaggio, Breughel, Rubens, Rembrandt, Poussin, Botticelli, Raphael, Titian, Giorgione, Tintoretto, Van Eyck all embellish this superb collection. Perhaps the most moving are the two halls devoted to Rembrandt; other high points include the Middle Ages section generally, the Renaissance in Italy, Germany and the Netherlands, and the sections on French and Rococo painting.

SKULPTURENGALERIE
Sculpture Gallery
Lansstraße 8, 1000 Berlin 33, Telephone 830 1248
Open Tuesday-Sunday 9-5. Closed Monday.
Underground Dahlem Dorf
This is West Germany's finest collection of sculpture. The range is extraordinary; including early Christian Byzantine, German Gothic, Italian sculpture from the Middle Ages through to the Baroque, French 18th century sculpture and European 19th century sculpture. Quite captivating are the miniatures about — 300 in all — from the 16th century to the 18th inclusive.

KUPFERSTICHKABINETT
Prints and Drawings Collection
Animallee 23/27, 1000 Berlin 33, Telephone 83011
Open Tuesday-Sunday 9-5; Studiensaal open Tuesday-Friday 9-4. Both closed Monday.
Underground: Dahlem Dorf.
Most of the prints and drawings collection is stored in the Studiensaal, the study-room, and a new exhibition is chosen from this store every three months or so. One can request to see the stored works from the staff in the Studiensaal; a choice ranging from etchings and prints from the 15th century to the present, drawings from the 14th century until the end of the 18th, lithographs from the 18th century onward, book illustrations from the 15th century through to contemporary examples, sketch books from the 16th century until the 19th century, screen prints, engravings and a typographical collection. One may like to request, for instance, Botticelli's Dante illustrations, engravings by Holbein or Dürer, or drawings and etchings by Rembrandt. The staff are very helpful; take care how one handles the works... it's

an exceptional collection. Note that the Studiensaal is only open from Tuesday-Friday 9-4pm whereas exhibitions are open at the normal times of Tuesday-Sunday 9-5pm.

MUSEUM FÜR DEUTSCHE VOLKSKUNDE
Museum of German Folklore

Im Winkel 6/8, 1000 Berlin 33, Telephone 832031.
Open Tuesday-Sunday 9-5. Closed Monday.
Underground: Dahlem Dorf.
A museum that shows the care and creativity of centuries which made up the traditions of the German household and daily way of life, especially of the 'ordinary folk'. On display are fascinating collections of furniture, utensils, textiles (including lace-work, crochet, embroidery, and the famous 'blue printing'), clothing, jewellery and all kinds of examples of daily life in a German home. A section on religious life is also included.

The museum covers the period from the 16th century until the present but most of the objects are from the 18th or 19th centuries. There is a liveliness and warmth used in the methods of display appropriate to this feast of cultural history.

MUSEUM FÜR INDISCHE KUNST
Museum of Indian Art

Lansstraße 8, 1000 Berlin 33, Telephone: 8301438
Open Tuesday-Sunday 9-5. Closed Monday.
Underground: Dahlem Dorf
Quite magical amongst this haunting collection are the wall paintings dated at around the birth of Christ, yet which have hardly needed restoration. The displays, sensitively set against a black back-drop, include Turfan frescoes from the sixth to the 10th centuries depicting Buddhist legends; sculptures and miniatures of pre and early Indian history; art from Tibet, Nepal, India, Indonesia and Turkestan. Altogether deserving of its fame as the best collection of Indian art in Germany.

Exhibition Berlin 1900 at the Academy of Fine Arts

MUSEUM FÜR OSTASIATISCHE KUNST
Museum of East-Asian Art

Lansstraße 8, 1000 Berlin 33, Telephone 830 1438
Open Tuesday-Sunday 9-5. Closed Monday.
Underground: Dahlem Dorf.
This is a beautiful collection appropriately displayed with an atmosphere enhancing the serenity of the art of this part of the world. The works shown are mainly from China and Japan, dating from 3000 B.C. to the present. Because the collection is larger than the space available the selection of paintings and wood cuts changes every few months. Chinese carpets and porcelain, models of actors in costume set on a stage and the display of Japanese paintings and woodcuts are only some of the highlights offered.

MUSEUM FÜR ISLAMISCHE KUNST
Museum of Islamic Art

Lansstraße 8, 1000 Berlin 33, Telephone 830 1438
Open Tuesday-Sunday 9-5. Closed Monday.
Underground: Dahlem Dorf
What strikes one immediately about the Islamic collection is the impact of colour radiated by the hanging carpets. Book illustrations, reliefs, pottery, are some of the other highlights.

The Junior Museum and the Museum for the Blind

Lansstraße 8, 1000 Berlin 33.
Open Tuesday-Sunday 9-5. Closed Monday.
Underground: Dahlem Dorf.
Downstairs from the main foyer of the Dahlem Museums (Lansstraße) are two rooms set aside for exibitions, one for idesa and themes especially chosen for childen and another with exhibits able to be enjoyed by blind people. The exhibitions change periodically.

CHARLOTTENBURG MUSEUMS

ÄGYPTISCHES MUSEUM
Egyptian Museum

Schloßstraße 70, 1000 Berlin 19, Telephone 3201 267
Open Saturday-Thursday 9-5. Closed Friday
Underground: Richard-Wagner-Platz
Here one can see Berlin's Mona Lisa, the original bust of Queen Nefertiti, the beautiful, finely formed slender face which has become a timeless symbol of human beauty.
Berlin's Egyptian collection is one of the oldest in Eurcpe, begun in 1698 by order of Friedrich III. The museum was officially opened in 1828. On display is a breathtaking collection of ancient sculpture, reliefs, bronze and terracotta figures, jewellery and a papyrus collection spanning from pre-history until the Roman Empire.

Showroom of the Antiken Museum

ANTIKENMUSEUM
Museum of Antiquities

Schloßrraße 1, 1000 Berlin 19. Telephone 320 1216
Open Saturday-Thursday 9-5. Closed Friday
Underground: Richard-Wagner-Platz, then bus 54.

During World War II the Berlin collection of Green and Roman antiquities was hidden underground and after the war what was on each 'side' of Berlin remained there. This museum's collection is thus the complement to East Berlin's antiquities collection in the Pergamon Museum

The vase paintings, the Hellenistic terracotta statues from Priene, not to mention the coins, portraits, tableware and sculpture from ancient Greece and Rome from about 2000 B.C. to 100 A.D. together make this collection one of the most beautiful and inspiring in Europe. If one can dare choose, it is perhaps the ancient Roman jewellery which stills any sense of time.

MUSEUM FÜR VOR UND FRÜGESCHICHTE
Museum of Pre and Proto History

Schloß Charlottenburg, West Wing, Langhansbau. Telephone 320. 1233
Open Saturday-Thursday 9-5. Closed Friday.
Underground. Richard-Wagner-Platz, then bus 54
A museum about pre and early history of Europe and Asia Minor, older and middle Stone age cultures, early Stone age, the Bronze age and the early and late Iron ages.

GIPSFORMEREI
Plaster Moulding Shop

Sophie-Charlotten-Straße 17/18, 1000 Berlin 19, Telephne 321 7011
Open Monday-Friday 9-4. Closed weekends.

Underground Richard-Wagner-Platz, then bus 54
Copies of sculptures of all cultures are made here, shipped in
white or exact replicas. The copies are for sale.

NEUE NATIONALGALERIE
The New National Gallery

Potsdamer Straße 50, 1000 Berlin 30, Telephone 266-6
Open TuesdaySunday 9-6. Closed Monday
Underground: Kurfürstendammn, then buses 24/29/48/75/83
The front entrance is immediately compelling with its fine, clear
lines created by the architect Mies van der Rohe and com-
plemented by the sculptures of George Rickey and Joannis
Avramodis. The buildng itself is a perfect monument to 20th cen-
tury art.

The New National Gallery is the continuation of the
Gemäldegalerie (Paintings Gallery) in Dahlem and houses 19th
and 20th century European painting and sculpture.

There is a strong section on 19th century German painting including works by Caspar David Friedrich, Schinkel, Walmüller and
Menzel; a variety of French Impressionists such as Renoir, Monet
and Manet; some Cubist works, for example by Picasso; a fine
collection of early 20th century Expressionism including works by
Kirchner, Nolde, Kokoschka, Beckmann and Munch; examples of
Futurism (Legér); Abstractionism (Klee, Mondrian, Rothko); as
well as an important focus on contemporary works. Exhibits are
rotated as the space does not allow all the collection to be shown
together. Special exhibitions are also held. Note the sculpture
garden at the back of the building.

KUNSTGEWERBMUSEUM
Museum of Arts and Crafts/Applied Arts

Tiergartenstraße 6, 1000 Berlin 30, Telephone 266-6

National Gallery, West Berlin, built by Mies van der Rohe

Open Tuesday-Sunday 9-5. Closed Monday
Underground Kurfürstenstraße, then buses 48/83/24/29/75
Despite major losses from the collection caused by the war, there is almost too much to be seen here and the sheer aesthetic delight of it all is itself an inspiration. The collection is now housed in a new and very spacious building (next to the Philharmonie) so be prepared for heavy walking.

The exhibits of European applied arts are arranged according to time spans such as the Middle Ages to the Reanaissance, the Renaissance, Baroque and Rococco, Art Deco, Bauhaus and contemporary and within these periods again exhibited according to materials, for example silver, glass, furniture etc. A main focus is porcelain. There is also a section on scientific instruments.

MUSIKINSTRUMENTEN-MUSEUM
Museum of Musical Instruments

Tiergartenstraße 1, 1000 Berlin 30, Telephone 254 810
Open Tuesday-Saturday 9-5, Sunday 10-5, closed Monday. Tours can be arranged.
Underground: Kurfürstenstraße, then buses 48 or 83/24/29/75
The new building for the Musical Instruments Museum is situated next to the Philharmonie and was designed by the same architect Professor Scharoun. It is a celebration of music — its interior beautifully reflecting the shape of the treble clef and of musical notation.

This outstanding collection, begun in 1888, includes a great variety of instruments and some painting and sculpture. One can follow through the history of string, wind, brass and percussion instruments, the development of the piano 'family' (its forerunners, the spinet and the clavichord, for instance, are among the most beautiful exhibits to be seen here), look at instruments used in church music, military music and folk music. There is also a section on music publishing and music theory and to bring things right up to date, even a section on music and technology.

Cards, postcards and books are on sale; and there is a delightful cafe which at times also holds readings and cabaret.

BAUHAUS ARCHIV

Kligelhöferstraße 14, 1000 Berlin 30, Telephone 302611618
Closed Tuesday, open every other day from 11-5. Library and archives open Monday-Friday 1-1pm
Underground: Nollendorfplatz, buses 9/16/24/29/69
The Bauhaus Archiv is appropriately housed in a beautiful building designed from plans by Gropius. Its collection covers the history of the Bauhaus group from 1919-1933 in Weimar and Dessau, showing the ideas, work and continuing influences through paintings, drawings, models, household and industrial articles, furniture, and documents such as letters, manuscripts and photos. One can see, for instance, the architectural and furnishing plans of Gropius or Mies van der Rohe and the original model of the Dessau Bauhaus; and works by Klee, Kandinsky, Ludwig Hirschfeld-Mack, Moholy-Nagy, Schlemmer and other participants of the school, including works by pupils.

The library contains around 9000 volumes. Alternating exhibitions are invariably of high quality and interest. Also a pleasant cafe in which to enjoy a break.

BERLIN MUSEUM

Lindenstraße 14, 1000 Berlin 61, Telephone 251 4015
Open Tuesday-Sunday 11-6pm. Closed Monday.
Underground: Hallesches Tor. Buses 24/29/41/75/95
This glorious old gold building stands strongly amidst the bare scenes of old and new, typical of Berlin, and especially this part of Kreuzberg. The museum shows exhibits conveying Berlin's tempestuous history, concentrating on the 17th century until today. The numerous paintings and drawings displayed throughout the different sections are worthy of a gallery alone. Recreations of sitting-rooms, examples of fashion, much porcelain, some glass, uses of silver, iron and wood, a lovely section on children's toys which tops the building and ones feeling of being able to live Berlin's history for a few hours, many documents and photos, models of Berlin's planning and architecture at different times and a room devoted to the Jewish community's history in Berlin are some of the sections which make up this phenomenal museum. Last but not least is the Alt-Berliner-Weißbierstube (Old Berlin White-beer Pub) which serves, of course, the famous beer and tasty inexpensive food in an intimate atmosphere of 'old Berlin'. Both museum and pub are not to be missed!

BERLINISCHE GALERIE

Gropius-Bau, Stresemanstraße 110, Berlin 61
Open Wednesday, Friday, Saturday, Sunday 10-18, Thursday 12-8pm.
Underground Kreuzberg.
Although called a gallery this is actually a unique and very important museum which not only exhibits but also collects Berlin art, with the one exception of work by the group Die Brücke which are housed in their own museums. The collection ranges from around 1870 until the present with a threefold emphasis: the art of Berlin at the turn of this century; the 1920's; contemporary art. It serves therefore as the link between the Berlin Museum and the Neue Nationalgalerie. The artists represented may or may not be Berliners, but the works were all created in Berlin, the aim being not only to build a collection of the fine arts and architecture of 19th and 20th century Berlin but also to show the collection in the context of Berlin's development as a city. Works suppressed by the Nazis are also being gathered from world-wide sources.

The collection is made up of paintings, sculpture, drawings, prints, architectural archives, and photos. Due to restricted space in the Jebenstraße building only a fraction was displayed at one time. The move to the Martin-Gropius-Bau in 1986 has solved this problem; the space there is 13 times that of the present gallery.

BRÖHAN-MUSEUM

Schloßstraße 1a, 1000 Berlin 19, Telephone 321.4029
Open Tuesday-Sunday 10-6pm. Closed Monday.
Underground: Richard-Wagner-Platz, then bus 54; or underground

Sophie-Charlotte-Platz and bus 74.
For fans of Art Nouveau and Art Deco this is a must. The museum is divided into different rooms, most of which are named after a well known European furniture company. Porcelain, glass, silver, furniture, paintings and sculpture are displayed in a way that they were originally used so that moving from "salon" to "salon" one moves through different ways of living and different eras. The painting and sculpture include works by Hans Baluschek, Karl Hagemeister, Willy Jaeckel and Jean Lambert-Rucki. There are also some interesting examples of industrial design of the period. There are also special exhibitions, such as the exhibition of Rosenthal porcelain.

BRÜCKE-MUSEUM

Bussardsteig 9, 1000 Berlin 33, Telephone 831 2029
Closed Tuesday, Open every other day from 11-5
Underground: Oscar-Helene-Heim, bus 60 to and from Wittenbergplatz. (To reach the museum get out at the Pückler Straße stop and follow the signs).
The museum, set amidst a luscious outlook of trees, was designed by Werner Düttman, the architect of the Akademie der Künste building. It has a deep serenity, an effective contrasting backdrop to the colour and tempestuousness of the works on display.
   The Brücke Museum, named after the artists' group Die Brücke of 1905-1913, displays works by the masters of German Expressionism; Bleyl, Heckel, Karl Schmidt-Rotluff (who gave to Berlin his own collection of paintings which set the foundation for this museum), Kirchner, Müller, Nolde and Pechsteim. One or two exhibitions are held each year from the collection not on display and at times special exhibitions are also held. It is a stimulating museum worthy of the artists who were its inspiration.

FLUXUS MUSEUM

Knesebeckstraße 76, 1000 Berlin 12, Telephone 883 4037
Open Monday-Friday 4-7pm, Saturday 11-2
Underground Uhlanstraße/Buses 29/19/9
This is a museum about 'fluxus' art showing works by international artists, mainly from Germany and Europe, about half from the United States, some works also from Eastern Europe. Artists include Vostell, Dick Higgins, Alison Knowles, Milon Knizak.

GEORG-KOLBE-MUSEUM

Sensburger Allee 25, 1000 Berlin 19, Telephone 304 2144
Open Tuesday-Sunday 10-5. Closed Monday. (Note: ring the bell to enter).
Bus 92/94 from Zoologische Garten to Preußenallee
Housed in the house of sculptor Georg Kolbe (1877-1947), the most well-known German sculptor of the 1920's and 30's, the museum is devoted mainly to Kolbe's works. The sculptures are on display in what was originally his studio and in the garden which the studio looks out on. On display are also a few works by Kolbe's contemporaries, Scheibe, Blumenthal and Sintenis for example, and paintings by his friends Rotluff and Kirchner. At times

the museum also holds special exhibitions.

OTHER MUSEUMS AND COLLECTIONS

BERLINER POST-und FERNMELDEMUSEUM
Berlin Museum of the postal service and communications technology.

Kleiststraße 13, 1000 Berlin 30, Telephone 212.8201, entrance: An der Urania.
Open Tuesday-Friday 10-4, Saturday and Sunday 10-1. Closed Monday.
Underground: Wittenbergplatz, buses 19/29/69/73/85
This museum has an individuality and a directness well suited to the comprehensive choice of examples tracing the history of the postal service and communications' technology. The history of the telegraph, telephone, television and the mail service are all there: the first telephone of 1881 is a highlight as is the extraordinary range of old post boxes.

BOTANISHES MUSEUM
Botanical Museum

Unter den Eichen 5-37, 1000 Berlin 45/Konigen-Luise-Straße 6-8, 1000 Berlin 33, Telephone 831 4041.
Open Tuesday-Sunday 10-5, Wednesday 10-6, Closed Monday.
Buses 1/48/68/85.
This museum is over 100 years old and is the only botaical museum in West Germany. The history, topology, preparation, growth and reproduction of plants are explained through displays of plants, diagrams and models. The library is open on the same days as the museum but from 9-3pm only.

BOTANISCHE GARTEN
Botanical Garden

Address as above
Open daily from 9-8pm; glass-houses 9-5.15 and on Sunday from 10-5.15
Next door to the museum is the Botanical Garden first created in 1679 in Schöneberg and laid out between 1897 and 1903 in Dahlem-Lichterfelde. One can enjoy walking along the grand wide paths or through romantic tracks graced by trees and plants planted as if in their natural surroundings. More stylised flower-beds provide a contrast and the glass-houses are outstanding. The Botanical Garden is a place of information about 18,000 or so different plants, one of the larger selections in Europe, as well as simply being a beautiful park to enjoy.

MUSEUM FÜR VERKEHR UND TECHNIK
Museum of Transport and Technology

Trebbiner Straße 9, 1000 Berlin 61, Telephone 25484-0
Open Tuesday, Wednesday, Friday, Saturday and Sunday from 10-6, Thursday 10-10pm. Closed Monday.

Underground: Gleisedreieck/Möckernbrücke, buses 29/75.
Housed in the building of the old Anhalter Station, this museum is devoted to the development of transport and technology. The museum itself is continually developing and further plans are already underway, for example a complete re-creation of a railway workshop is to be opened in time for Berlin's 750 years celebration in 1987. Now, most imaginatively displayed, one can see a variety of means of transport; bicycles, motor vehicles, aeroplanes, model boats; a section on the history of printing (with demonstrations of the presses) a section on the history of typewriters and numerous examples of technlogy with explanations of its connection to the basis of physics. A visit will increase your appetite — fortunately there's a museum cafe-restaurant next door!

KRIMINAL MUSEUM

Platz der Luftbrücke, Tempelhof, Telephone 6991.
Open Monday 2-3pm
Underground: Platz der Luftbrücke
A museum for those interested in criminal investigation, with the focus on Berlin. However one must be 16 years or over to enter. Group tours can be arranged by telephone.

ANTI-KRIEGS-MUSEUM
Anti-War Museum

Genter Straße 9, 1000 Berlin 65, Telephone 461. 7837/402.8691
Open 4-8pm everyday.
Underground: Leopold Platz
This is a private, collectively run museum in the tradition of Quaker pacifism. Ernst Friedrich founded the first anti-war museum which was smashed by the Nazis and Ernst Friedrich himself was forced to flee to London. His grandson Mr Spree now runs this not only most interesting but incalculably worthwhile museum.

DEUTSCHES RUNDFUNKMUSEUM
German Radio Museum

Hammarskjöldplatz 1, 1000 Berlin 19, Telephne 302 8186
Open Wednesday-Monday from 10-5. Closed Tuesday
Underground: Kaiserdamm/Theodor-Heuss-Platz
A museum devoted to the history of the German radio, from 1920 to present. The history of television will also be a part of the museum in the future.

HAUS AM CHECKPOINT CHARLIE

Friedrichstraße 44, 1000 Berlin 61, Telephone 251.4569/251.6902
Open everyday 9-8pm.
Underground Friedrichstraße
Photos, films, artefacts and paintings about the division between East and West Berlin can be seen here. The museum has also formed an association and publishing house.

Martin Gropius Building

BERLIN PAVILLION

Straße des 17 Juni am S bahnhof Tiergarten, Telephone 391.7951
Open 11-7pm everyday except Monday
S-Bahn Tiergarten.
Exhibitions of old Berlin street furniture, those lovely old gas
lamps for example, as well as exhibitions about Berlin's history
and town planning. The Pavillion has been created in the style of
an old-Berlin pub.

PALACES AND GARDENS

Schloß Charlottenburg

Luisenplatz, 1000 Berlin 19, Telephone 32011.
Open Tuesday-Sunday 9-5pm, Wednesday 9-7pm Closed Monday.
Buses: 9,21,54,62,74,87,
(Closest underground Richard-Wagner-Platz or Sophie-Charlotte-
Platz).
Schloß Charlottenburg is a successful blend of grandeur and
delicacy. It is imposing and complemented by a beautiful park. In
addition to the palace the Orangeries, the Schinkel Pavilion, the
Belvedere and the Mausoleum are separate buildings in the
grounds, each with its own history and atmosphere.

Through the main entrance of the Schloß, and you are immediately confronted with the richness and light of this former
Prussian monarch's home. Note the juxtaposition of historical
and contemporary with the modern abstract painting on the ceiling above the stairs. The Golden Gallery is a stunning example of
German Rococo, an interweaving of light and reflections achieved
through the use of mirrors and gold. Paintings, including works by
Watteau, Lancret and Peine, furniture, tapestries and porcelain
adorn these rooms.

The living apartments of Sophie Charlotte can only been seen with a guide (usually you wait a short while for a group to form — no need to book in advance). These rooms are darker and heavier in style than the rest of the Schloß and one could say, on occasion, even a little eccentric, for example, the Chinese porcelain room. There is much to see: paintings of the royal family, among others, furniture, the Baroque tapestries Sophie Charlotte was so fond of, the use of wood and arrangement of colours. The tour gives one a good insight into the atmosphere of court and the daily life of the monarchy.

Altogether different is the Schinkel Pavilion, built by Schinkel in 1825 as a summerhouse for Friedrich Wilhelm 111 and his morganatic wife Augusta Fürsten von Liegnitz. It is elegant, intimate and demure in atmosphere, each room with its own individuality produced by a particular colour and theme. Drawings, sketches and paintings by Schinkel and paintings by Caspar David Friedrich feature, as well as a comprehensive selection of early 19th century paintings.

The Belvedere (tea-house), set deeper into the park amongst the trees and itself a strikingly original building, contains the historical porcelain collection. Here one winds up through a spiral staircase connecting three floors of exquisite porcelain made by Berlin manufacturers.

Open only in the summer, the Mausoleum exhibits memorials of the royal family. Note the sarcophagus of Königen Luise by Rauch.

The Große Orangerie (large Orangery) has been restored and is used for special exhibitions. To complete an enjoyable experience sit and eat well in the Kleine Orangerie (small Orangery), once the gardeners' quarters and now a very good restaurant.

Jagdschloß Grunewald
Hunting Lodge in Grunewald

Grunewaldsee, Telephone 813.3596.
Open Tuesday-Sunday 10-4. Closed Monday.
Buses 1/60/68.

The Jagdschloß is a Renaissance style hunting lodge built in 1542 and rebuilt in 1700. Set in the woods, overlooking a lake its enchanting setting is worthy of a Hans Christian Andersen or Grimm fairy-story. On display in the lodge are about 200 masterpieces by German, Dutch and Flemish painters, including several by Lucas Cranach, as well as furniture, porcelain, glass and of course hunting equipment and weapons including the hunting collection of Prince Karl von Preußen.

Schloß und Park Kleinglienicke
Wansee, Telephone 805.4000
Bus 6.

The buildings of this one-time summer residence of Prince Karl von Preußen, designed by Schinkel, are distinctive for their clear beauty of line and as rare examples in West Berlin today of the early classical period. Complementing the architecture are the beautiful and elegantly landscaped grounds. Although you can only view the buildings from the outside a visit to the Wansee royal residence is a delight which should not be missed, for it is one of the most beautiful spots in West Berlin.

Schloß Bellevue
Spreeweg. Tiergarten
Telephone 391051.
Bus 23 stops right outside.

Schloß Bellevue is now the residence of the West German President when he is in West Berlin and is therefore only open (best to phone to arrange a tour) to the public when he and his wife are not in residence. The palace was built 200 hundred years ago in 1785 in a classical style, modelled after the French Baroque palaces. After the Second World War it had to be completely restored, so

Glienicke Castle by Schinkel

that now the interior is not as it was originally but the restoration in the Empire style (with a few 1950's additions!). A beautiful park, always open to the public when the President is not in West Berlin, lies behind the palace.

Schloß Pfaueninsel
Pfaueninsel (Peacock Island)
Schloß, Telephone 805.3042.
Open 10-5 everyday except Monday.
No. 6 bus or a special, No. 907 to the island from Wansee station, then a half-minute ferry ride across the island.
You can only view the interior of the Schloß as part of a tour but there is no need to book; one tour follows another.

Riehmers Hofgarten, Kreuzberg 1893

The Pfaueninsel — Peacock Island — is a delightful natural reserve where you can walk, picnic, simply relax and enjoy the peacocks, not to mention the fresh air, as well as view the buildings on the island; the most interesting being the Schloß.

This was built as the summer residence of Kaiser Frederich 111 and his wife Louise. The wooden building, highly original in style and made to look like a theatrical ruin, is 188 years old.

Much of the interior is not restored and you can therefore gain a clear picture of the palace as it once was. There are several distinctive features: for instance the use of mahogany; the differently designed and hand-made wooden floors of each room; the hand-painted wooden mirror frames; the wall-papers (then a new phenomenon) and wall fabrics; the circular reading room with rounded window and door frames to complement, and the same room's wall-painting of the South Seas, then in fashion. The 'entertaining' room is lined with beautifully panelled wooden walls. Its ceiling paintings are copies by Johann Christoph Frisch of Guido Reni's Aurora in the Palazzo Rospigliosi in Rome and Annibale Carracci's Ganymed, Apollo and Hyacinth in Palazzo Farnese in Rome.

Note also in the same room the 1780 piano which is one of six of its type in the world. Last but not least — *the* novelty of the time — one of the first European lavatories, proudly on display in the dressing room.

Other buildings on the island include the Cavalier House, the dairy and the Queen Luise Memorial Temple.

Schloß Tegel
Adelheidallee 19-21, Tegel, Telephone 434.3156.
Open only on Sunday from 2-5, tours about hourly (one can only view the Schloß as part of a tour).
Underground: Tegel, Buses: 13,14,15,20.

This former Renaissance country-house was rebuilt by Schinkel for the von Humboldt family in the 1820's to complement their collection of casts of antique sculptures. Various living-rooms from the von Humboldt's summer residence, as it was then used, can be seen, also their library and sitting room for instance, each with paintings of the family lining the walls.

PLACES OF ARCHITECTURAL INTEREST

Included below are places not already described in the Guide and which are of interest from an architectural perspective.

Kaiser-Friedrich-Gedächtnis-Kirche In the centre of the city area; one can't miss it. Note the contrast between the 1893-95 war-damaged church and its twin of 1957.

Hebbel Theater Stresemannstraße 29.

Riemers Hofgarten, Yorckstraße, Hagelbergstraße, Großbeerenstraße (different entrances, all in Kreuzberg).

Hansaviertel, Straße des 17 Juni. An example of 1950's architecture; apartment blocks designed by different architects as part of an international competition held then.

Reichstagsgebäude, Platz der Republik. The Parliament House of former monarchical times, and the Weimar Republic, now used as exhibition halls.

St. Matthäus-Kirche, Matthäikirchplatez. Of the Schinkel school.

Dorfkirche, Alt-Marienfeld. The oldest church in Berlin, dated at 1220.

Jüdisches Gemeindezentrum, Fasanenstraße 79-80. The new Jewish Community Centre built adjoining the old entrance of the pre-war Synagogue.

Le-Corbusier-Haus, Reichssportfelderstraße 16.

St. Annen-Kirche, Königen-Luise-Straße. Example of backstein. Dated from 13th/14th centuries; with additions.

Mittelhof, Kirchweg 33, Nikolassee. Hermann Muthesius, built 1914-15.

St. Nikolai-Kirche, Reformationplatz. Possibly 1210.

ART INSTITUTES

AKADEMIE DER KÜNSTE

Hanseatenweg 10, 1000 Berlin 21, Telephone 391.1031
Open daily from 10-7pm except Monday which is open from 1-7pm and Friday open from 10am-9pm
Underground: Hansaplatz
President: Günter Grass
Secretary: Manfred Schlösser
Press: Klaus-Peter Herbach
The Akademie der Künste, or Academy of Arts, was recreated after the war, in 1954, and housed from 1960 on in a spacious, serene building designed by Werner Düttman. Like the Academie Francaise its membership is renowned and based world-wide, each member contributing to ideas for projects and the discussion of artistic matters. For the public it is an arts centre which presents important and new works of quality in all the arts.

The Academy's programme in Berlin has a thematic emphasis, the intention being to connect artistic expression to historical and cultural developments. The programme generally is of an exceptionally high standard and often provocative, and includes concerts, exhibitions, theatre, readings, lectures, films, some dance and at times performances. The Academy also organises and hosts discussion forums. A library and archives are on the premises.

DAAD
Deutscher Akademischer Austauschdienst, Berlin Künstlerprogramm

Salome at his Raab Gallery exhibition

German Academic Exchange Service, Artists-in-Berlin-Programme

Stinplatz 2, 1000 Berlin 12, Telephone 3100030
Director: Professor Wieland Schmidt
Underground: Zoo; Buses 23, 54, 55, 262, 73, 90, 92, 94.
The German Academic Exchange Service has a special programme for Berlin called the Artists-in-Berlin-Programme. Founded in 1963 it was, in its first two years, financed by the Ford Foundation and is now financed by the Berlin Senate and the DAAD in
Bonn. The programme includes five sections: the fine arts, music,
literature, architecture and film. The scheme invites non-German
artists to spend a year in Berlin on a grant covering living costs
(2900 DM monthly plus help for rent) and sometimes an apartment
or studio if necessary. A different jury for each section, chosen
afresh each year, decides who to invite from the applicants.
About 20-25 artists are chosen.

   The works created in the year are shown or performed in Berlin,
often in the DAAD Gallery at Kurfürstenstraße 58, which is open
daily from midday to 7pm. Concerts and readings are also held
there. The DAAD's contacts with other institutions, such as the
Akademie der Künste, the Literansches Collequium or the Neue
Nationalgalerie are important and combined events and exhibitions are often organised.

   For those interested in applying for the Artists in Berlin Programme, write to ask for the application form: Berliner Künstlerprogramm: Informationen und Heinweise/Artists in Berlin Programme: Information and Remarks, the address as above. Note
the juries decide each March-April for the following year.

KÜNSTLERHAUS BETHANIEN

Mariannenplatz 2, 1000 Berlin 36, Telephone 614.8010/01
Director: Dr. Michael Haerdter

Underground: Görlitzer Bahnhof

Künstlerhaus Bethanien, financed by the Berlin Senate, is the most significant arts centre for artists to work in, offering to artists of different nationalities the space, materials and encouragement for projects in architecture, film, graphics, literature, music, painting, performance, photography, sculpture, theatre and video. It is the main place for artists' studios in Berlin.

Artists are usually chosen for a year on the combined strength of their Curriculum Vitae and the project on which they propose to work. There are 24 studios or rehearsal rooms available, 50% of which are reserved for DAAD artists.

A variety of exhibitions, concerts, readings, films, theatre productions as well as workshops and seminars are open to the general public.

The Druckwerkstatt/Printing Workshop.

Address as above, Telephone 614.2027
Also at the Künstlerhaus, though independent of it (administered by the Berufsverband Bildener Künstler) is the Druckwerkstatt, a workshop with facilities for lithography, etchings, silk-screening, book printing and binding, off set printing, photographic reproduction and woodcuts. Artists are accepted on the strength of a Hochschule der Künste diploma, membership of the BBK or on the quality of their work. Although the workshop is meant for Berliners only, special arrangements for BRD or international artists are not ruled out. Artists need only to pay for materials. About 100 artists use the facilities each year.

INTERNATIONALES DESIGN ZENTRUM BERLIN e.v.

Wielandstraße 31, 1000 Berlin 12, Telephone 882. 3051
Director: Dr Angela Schönberger
Underground: Uhlandstraße

Kunstlerhaus Bethanien — Raffael Rheinsberg with his installation "See with your hands".

The Internationales Design Zentrum — The International Design Centre — was founded in 1969. Its purpose is to display to the public different examples of international design and to hold seminars, conferences and forums about design to further the general awareness of the aesthetic, sociological, technical, economic and industrial aspects of design.

Several exhibitions and a programme of information and discussion are held throughout the year: telephone or write to the above address for information.

STATE FINANCED GALLERIES

STAATLICHE KUNSTHALLE BERLIN

Budapester Straße 46, 1000 Berlin 30, Telephone 261.7067/8
Open Tuesday-Sunday 10-6, Wednesday 10-10. Closed Monday.
Underground: Zoologischer Garten
Director: Dieter Ruckhaberle
Founded in 1977, this is Berlin's City Gallery showing a different exhibition every six to eight weeks. Four directions are prominent: the showing of works by Berlin artists; exhibiting works by German artists suppressed or forced to emigrate by the Nazis; showing exhibitions by international artists; thematic exhibitions for example the Kunsthalle has shown an exhibition about Art and the Media or another entitled The Road to Dictatorship. Exhibitions at the Kunsthalle are of a high standard and often provocative.

NEUE GESELLSCHAFT FÜR BILDENDE KUNST

Tempelhofer Ufer 22, 1000 Berlin 61, Telephone 216.3047
Open Monday-Friday 10-5

Exhibition 5 Situations in 5 rooms at the Kunstquartier Ackerstrasse

Underground: Mockernbrücke

Like the Neue Berliner Kunstverein this is an art organisation and gallery financed by the Berlin Senate. Inspired by the student movement of the '60's decisions are made by members, the decision-making thereby motivated from the base rather than directed by committee above. Exhibitions are usually chosen to show art in a historical-political context. One of the aims of the NGBK is to provide a place for questioning, critical art. The association has a special interest in 'political art' and socialist themes portrayed in art.

NEUER BERLINER KUNSTVEREIN

Kurfürstendamm 58, 1000 Berlin 15. Telephone 323.7091/93
Open Monday and Friday 12-6.30, Tuesday and Thursday 12-8, Saturday 11-4
Underground: Kurfürstendamm

Like the NGBK the NBK is also financed by the Senate but differently organised in that its decision-making is initiated by a director and committee. Exhibitions are mainly by Berlin artists. One can loan paintings and sculpture from the Artothek and video art from the videothek. The Kunstverein also displays works bought by the Senate and has been an important motivator of significant Berlin exhibitions, for instance the Zeitgeist exhibition.

PRIVATE GALLERIES

Abend-Galerie Ursule Noé

Heilbronner Straße 13, 1000 Berlin 30, Telephone 211.6163
Director: Ursula Noé
No fixed direction, although interest in contemporary abstractionism and Pop Art. Specialises in Swiss artists.
Open Monday-Friday 4-8, Saturday 11-2.
Underground: Bayerischer Platz

AGO-Galerie

Meierottostraße 1, 1000 Berlin 15, Telephone 881. 9024
Director: Wolfgang Thiede
Particular interest in German art from the eighteenth century until 1950. Emphasis, in this century, on the November Gruppe, Neue Sachlichkeit and Expressionism.
Open Tuesday-Friday 2-6.30, Saturday 10-2
Underground: Spichernstraße

Art Work Galerie Neumann

Mommsenstraße 62, 1000 Berlin 12, Telephone 883. 8785
Director: Ms Neumann
A gallery showing works by young Berlin artists, mostly by those who have recently completed their Hochschule der Künste study.
Open Wednesday-Friday 7-9, Saturday 11-2
Underground Uhlandstraße

Artificium

Beusselstraße 86, 1000 Berlin 21, Telephone 345.4925
Director: Joachim Weidler.
Mainly living West Berlin artists and emphasis on the traditional realistic or expressionistic modes. Mr Weidler combines young and well-known artists so that the former receive the spin-off from the public's interest in the latter. Also antiques and crafts.
Open Tuesday-Friday 2-6.30, Saturday 11-1.30.
Underground: Turmstraße.

Atelier für Polnische Kunst

Dorfstraße 57, 1000 Berlin 20, Telephone 331.6688
Director: Mr Skorupski
Shows contemporary Polish painting, sculpture, graphics and glass work. Mr Skorupski also organises exhibitions of Polish art in other galleries. By appointment.
Underground: Rathaus Spandau.

Ben Wargin-Baumpaten e.V.

Studio: Joseph-Haydn-Straße 1, 1000 Berlin 21.
Presentation: Ackerstraße 71, 1000 Berlin 65.
Telephone: 463.4099/392.6049.
Room installations by artist Ben Wargin and team. At least three exhibitions each year, sometimes presented elsewhere depending upon appropriate space.
By appointment.
Joseph-Haydn-Straße: S-Bahn Tiergarten.
Ackerstraße: Bus 90 from Zoologische Garten.

Bildhauergalerie Plinthe

Grolmanstraße 46, 1000 Berlin 12, Telephone 883.2285
Director: Mr Grosch.
Specialises in smaller sculptures, mainly by living German sculptors.
Open Thursday, Friday, Saturday 3-6.30
Underground: Uhlandstraße.

Daad Galerie

Kurfürstenstraße 58, 1000 Berlin 30, Telephone 261.3640.
Director: Professor Wieland Schmied, Rene Block.
Mostly exhibitions of work by artists on DAAD scholarships. Readings and concerts etc are also held there, given also by scholarship holders.
Open daily 12-7
Underground: Kurfürstenstraße/Nollendorfplatz.

Deplankunsthalle

Kurfürstendamm, Güterbahnhof, Halensee, 1000 Berlin 31. Telephone 892 5157
Director: Mr Wolfgang Schegger

Elvira Back in her studio in Kreuzberg

Changing exhibitions
Open daily 3-7, except Mondays.
S-Bahn Halansee. Buses 19 and 29.

Elefanten Press Galerie

Zossener Straße 32, 1000 Berlin 61. Telephone 693 7026
Collective led by Tom Fecht, a gallery and a publishing house. Art in the context of cultural and political themes, historical and contemporary. Interest in the 'alternative scene'.
Open Monday-Saturday 11-6.30, Sunday and holidays 12-5.
Underground: Gneisenaustraße.

Förtsch Galerie

Pfalzburger Straße 12, 1000 Berlin 15, Telephne 881.7185.
Director: Sergej Förtsch.
Contemporary painting, photography, painting with photography, sculpture. Artists include: Carola Devur, Robert Schad, Hermann Spörel, Peter Werner.
Open Wednesday-Friday 3-7, Saturday 11-6.
Underground: Spichernstraße/Hohenzollerndamm.

Frauengalerie Andere Zeichen

Bleibtreustraße 53, 1000 Berlin 12, Telephone 313 8991.
Director: Ms Sakel
One criterion — only women artists exhibited. Readings, music, films also shown. Closed to men, except on Sundays!
Open Wednesday-Sunday 4-7
Underground: Uhlandstraße.

Galerie Aedes

Grolmanstraße 51, 1000 Berlin 12. Telephone 312 2598
Director: Christina Feireiff.
The only gallery in West Berlin exhibiting plans and models of architectural design and interiors. A wide variety of exhibitions, usually of avant-garde international architecture.
Open Tuesday-Friday 4-7, Saturday 11-2.
Underground: Zoologische Garten.

Galerie Alexandra

Bregenzer Straße 7, 1000 Berlin 15, Telephone 881 2494
Director: Alexandra Lange-Baihr
Opened March 1985, a new gallery with a focus on Expressionist painting especially of a Junge Wilden style but not exclusively.
Open Wednesday-Friday 6-8, Sunday 11-3
Underground: Adenauer Platz.

Galerie Andre, Anselm Dreher

Pfalzburger Straße 80, 1000 Berlin 15, Telephone 883.5249/796.5572
Director: Anselm Dreher
One of the most important galleries in West Berlin and one of the few with a special interest in abstractionism. The main focus is on conceptual art; installations and sculpture also feature. Work by artists from the Rhine area are regularly shown. Works by Karol Bethke, Jochen Fishcer, Imi Knoebel, Susanne Mahlmeister, Mechtild Nemeczek, Reiner Ruthenbeck and Eva-Maria Schön all shown 1985-86.
Open Tuesday-Friday 3-7.
Underground Spichernstraße/Uhlandstraße.

Galerie Antoine

Clausewitzstraße 6, 1000 Berlin 12, Telephone 883.4529
Director: Tony Stehlik.
Exhibits French artists, oil painting, lithography, usually representational. Artists include Daneis, Hemeret, Matallana, Mozziconacci, Perino, Satur.
Open Tuesday-Friday 10-1 and 3-7, Saturday 10-6.
Underground: Adenauer Platz.

Galerie Binhold

Kurfürstendamm 186, 1000 Berlin 15, Telephone 881. 1576
Director Mr Binhold
Concentration on the classical modern. Among others there are four exhibitions each year of the following: Chagall, Dali, Hamm, Miro and Picasso.
Open Monday-Friday 10-6.30, Saturday 10-2 (10-6 first Saturday of each month).
Underground: Adenauer Platz.

Galerie Bodo Niemann

Giesebrechtstraße 3, 1000 Berlin 12, Telephone 882.2620.
Director: Bodo Niemann.
Mainly German art of the 1920's expressing themes about city life, its loneliness and pressures for example. Mr Niemann is also interested in exhibiting less known classical modern artists, international artists and some contemporary art. Painting features.
Main artists are: Albert Birkle, Karl Hubbuch, Paul Kuhfuss, Bruno Voigt.
Open Wednesday-Friday 3-7, Saturday 11-4.
Underground: Wilmesdorfer Straße.

Galerie Bossen

Gersdorfstraße 62, 1000 Berlin 42, Telephone 705.9734
Director: Mr Bossen
Contemporary painting and sculpture. Also furniture, antiques, graphics, glass, pottery, silver and gold.
Open Tuesday-Friday 11-6, Saturday 10-1.
Underground: Walter-Schreiber-Platz, then bus 76 to Kaiser Straße stop.

Galerie Bossin

Meierottostraße 1, 1000 Berlin 15, Telephone 883. 2505
Director Herbert Bossin.
A rare gallery in West Berlin in that it is especially interested in constructivism and the 'geometric' in painting. Four major artists are regularly exhibited, exclusive in West Berlin, to this gallery: Badur, Max Bill, the Swiss artist who is a member of the Akademie der Künste as well as one of the few still living Bauhaus artists and who is now President of the Bauhaus Archiv, Raimund Girke, a monochrome painter, and Richard-Paul Lohse who explores an extension of Mondrian's concrete art. Other artists include Erich Bucholz, Johannes Geccelli and Kuno Gonschior.
Open Tuesday-Friday 3-6, Saturday 11-3.
Underground: Spichernstraße.

Galerie Bremer

Fasanenstraße 37, 1000 Berlin 15, Telephone 881.4908
Director: Rudolf van der Lak
Established straight after the war, in 1946, which makes it one of the oldest galleries in West Berlin, this gallery is renowned for being the first to show works by artists forbidden by the Nazis and for introducing Berliners to a variety of famous and then yet-to-be-discovered international artists. It also became, through its clubroom, a centre for artists and associates to meet. The gallery now shows three to four exhibitions each year, mainly by painters, including for instance, Bergmann, Hans Jaenisch, Küchenmeister and Rudolf Kügler. It also houses a fine selection of prints and exhibits the graphics and sculpture of Günter Grass,. After the death, in 1985, of Anja Bremer, her partner and husband Rudolf van der Lak, assumed single directorship.

Berlin gallery interior

Open Tuesday-Friday 10-1 and 4-6, Saturday 10-1. Apart from Sunday also open daily after 8pm.
Underground: Kurfürstendamm/Uhlandstraße.

Galerie Brigitte Wölfer

Kurfürstendamm 206, 1000 Berlin 15, Telephone 883.7153
Director: Brigitte Wölfer
Traditional gallery with a focus on naive painting
Open Tuesday-Friday 3-6, Saturday 11-2.
Underground: Uhlandstraße.

Galerie Brusberg

Kurfürstendamm 213, 1000 Berlin 15, Telephone 882.7682
Director: Dieter Brusberg
One of *the* galleries in West Berlin, created after its forerunner in Hannover. It is a highly successful gallery, very chic, and housed in a luscious 1890's building at the corner of Kurfürstendamm and Uhlandstraße. It specialises in twentieth century international art, especially the classical modern, surrealist, contemporary West Berlin art, and is one of the main galleries in West Berlin showing East German artists. Sculpture also features. Artists include Max Ernst, Fernand Léger, Pablo Picasso and, exclusive in West Berlin to Galerie Brusberg, Gerhard Attenbourg, Emil Cimiotti, Bernard Heisig and Rolf Szymanski.
Open Monday-Friday 10-1 and 2.30-6.30, Saturday 10-2.
Underground: Uhlandstraße.

Galerie Büsch

Glockenturmstraße 20a, 1000 Berlin 19, Telephone 304.1513.
Director: Ms Büsch

Mainly contemporary French and German painting. Landscapes a feature.
Open Tuesday-Friday 5-8.
Bus 92/94 from Zoologische Garten.

Galerie Butzer

Bozener Straße 13-14, 1000 Berlin 62, Telephone 853.7676
Director: Mr Butzer
A new gallery which opened in April 1985 exhibiting contemporary international artists.
Open Monday-Friday 2-7, Saturday 11-3.
Underground: Bayerische Platz.

Galerie am Chamissoplatz

Chamissoplatz 6, 1000 Berlin 61, Telephone 692.5381/693.1891
Collective of about 10 people led by Bernd Busch and Werner Tammen. Interest in a variety of media; painting, caricature, photography and focus on international contemporary art, mainly realist in orientation but not fixed. Exhibitions are often thematic and in the context of historical or socio-political ideas. The gallery is also a venue for cabaret, readings and concerts and shows a general interest in alternative art.
Open Tuesday-Friday 4-7, Saturday 2-6.
Underground: Gleisenauerstraße.

Galerie Dahlem Dorf

Königen-Luise-Straße 48, 1000 Berlin 33, Telephone 832 4560
Director: Ms Schirmacher
Main interests are traditional naturalistic painting and naive painting. Artists include Kurt Müllenhaupt and Hans Georg Rauchs. Annual pre-Christmas exhibition also displays pottery.
Open Tuesday-Friday 11-1 and 4-6.30, Saturday 11-2.
Underground: Dahlenm Dorf.

Galerie Eberhard Mönch

Damaschkestraße 22, 1000 Berlin 31, Telephone 323 9823
Director: Ederhard Mönch.
Concentration on abstract painting, especially by West Berlin and Stuttgart artists. Small sculptures also a feature. Mr Mönch is interested in young artists, not established artists.
Open Wednesday-Friday 4.30-7, Saturday 11-3.
Underground: Adenauer Platz.

Galerie 'el'

Lübecker Straße 26, 1000 Berlin 21, Telephone 396.6374
Partners Irmtraud Kewitz and Sieglinde Lüderetz.
Exhibitions of young international artists.
Open Monday-Friday 2-6.30, Saturday 11-2.
Underground: Birkenstraße.

Galerie Eremitage Berlin

Erdener Straße 4a, 1000 Berlin 33, Telephone 891.3158
Director: Ms Benjas
Shows painting, graphics, drawing, jewellery and pottery from Eastern Europe, mainly Soviet, Czech or Hungarian. Also organises exhibitions of West German art in Eastern Europe.
Open Monday-Friday 4-7, Sunday 11-3.
Bus: 19.

Galerie Eylau's

Eylauer Straße 5, 1000 Berlin 61, Telephone 786.3024/305.3236
Director: Norbert Pintch
Non-aligned. Contemporary painting and pottery.
Open Tuesday and Thursday 4-7
Underground: Kleistpark.

Galerie Fahnemann

Fasanenstraße 61, 1000 Berlin 15, Telephone 883.9897
Director: Clemens Fahnemann.
Although relatively new, just over two years old, this is one of the most important galleries in West Berlin, showing contemporary international painting, scupture, installations and photography. Emphasis on neo-expressionism. Among the artists: Frank Dornseif, Wilmar Koenig, Raimund Kummer, Rainer Mang, Bruce McLean, Ulaf Metze, Hermann Pitz, Reinhard Pods, Gerd Rohling, ter Hell, as well as small runs of exclusive prints by Elvira Bach, Peter Chevalier, Karl Horst Hödicke and A.R. Penck
Open Tuesday-Friday 2-6.30, Saturday 11-2.
Underground: Spichernstraße.

Galerie Folker Skulima

Niebuhrstraße 2, 1000 Berlin 12, Telephone 881.8280
Director: Folker Skulima. Partner Volker Dierl.
A significant gallery on the international art scene, taking part in art fairs at Basle, Chicago, Köln and Paris. The gallery focusses on the classical modern, especially Dada, the Bauhaus, Surrealism and Constructivism, as well as concentrating on contemporary painting and sculpture.
Open Tuesday-Friday 2-6, Saturday 10-2.
Underground: Kurfürstendamm.

Galerie Frohnau

Kasinoweg 7, 1000 Berlin 28, Telephone 401.4081/401.6758
Director: Ms Frohnau
Contemporary Berlin painting.
Open Wednesday, Thursday, Sunday 3-6.
Underground: Tegel.

Galerie Gärtner

Uhlandstraße 20-25, 1000 Berlin 12, Telephone 883.5385
Director: Peter Gärtner

Special interest in surrealist drawings. Large selection of lithographs and etchings of Berlin. Main artist Bruno Bruni.

Galerie Georg Nothelfer

Uhlandstraße 184, 1000 Berlin 12, Telephone 881.4405
Director: Georg Nothelfer
An established gallery mainly showing painting after 1945, specialising in the 'informal'. Artists include: Brosch, Galli, Stöhrer, Thieler, Voss, Zimmer.
Open Tuesday-Friday 2-6.30, Saturday 10-2.
Underground: Uhlandstraße
Mr Nothelfer also runs a smaller gallery in Riehmers Hofgarten, Hagelberger Straße 10c, 1000 Berlin 61, Telephone 785 5577. This gallery specialises in paper drawings by young artists.
Open Tuesday-Friday 3-7, Saturday 10-2.
Underground Mehringdamm, or bus 19.

Galerie Gerda Bassenge

Fasanenstraße 73, 1000 Berlin 15, Telephone 881.8104
Director: Gerda Bassenge
German, French and Italian etchings, lithographs, drawings, watercolours and maps from 1400 to the twentieth century classical moderns — works by Beckmann, Chagall, Dürer, Kollwitz, Liebermann, Nolde, Pechstein, Piranesi, Rembrandt. Also a comprehensive selection of historical Berlin drawings. An auction is held quarterly of art and books at the Bassenge auction house in Erdener Straße 5a, 1000 Berlin 33. The Fasanenstraße gallery is open Monday-Friday 10-6, Saturday 10-1.
Underground: Kurfürstendamm/Uhlandstraße.

Galerie Giannozzo

Suaretzstraße 28, 1000 Berlin 19, Telephone 321 7783
Director: Rolf Langebartels.
A unique gallery in West Berlin devoted exclusively to space-oriented installations and explorations into the relationship between space and sound.
Open Tuesday-Thurdsay 4-7, Saturday 3-6.
Underground: Sophie-Charlotte-Platz.

Galerie Hartwig

Knesebeckstraße 32, 1000 Berlin 12, Telephone 882.7115
Director: Mr Hartwig
Mainly contemporary Berlin painters and sculptors, for example Fussman, Hilsing, Meckel.
Open Tuesday-Friday 2-6.30, Saturday 10-2.
Underground: Uhlandstraße.

Galerie Horst Dietrich

Mommsentraße 57, 1000 Berlin 12, Telephone 324 5345
Director: Horst Dietrich
A gallery with a warm sparkle specialising in 'poetic realism' or

Karl Horst Hodicke the "father" of the New Fauves.

'lyrical realism' and showing mainly painting, drawing, sculpture, kinetic sculpture, textiles and, recently, an interest in the book as art work. Horst Dietrich places emphasis on art created by hand, that is without mechanical help. Artists shown include Hans Karl Busch, Barbara Fahrner, Berd Kastenholz and Wolf Spies.
Open Wednesday-Friday 4-7, Saturday 12-4.
Underground: Adenauer Platz.

Galerie am Havelufer

Imchenplatz 2, 1000 Berlin 22, Telephone 365.5281
Director: Elisabeth Hofmann
Traditional contemporary painting, sculpture, pottery.
Open Monday-Friday 4-7, Saturday 11-3.
From Wansee by boat or from Ruhleben with bus 34.

Galerie Kleber

Xantener Straße 5, 1000 Berlin 15, Telephone 883.9850
Director: Mr Kleber
Works by young painters, sometimes sculptors.
Open Monday-Friday 3-6. Saturday 11-1.
Underground: Adenauer Platz.

Galerie Kleines Kra

Fischerhüttenweg 67, 1000 Berlin 37, Telephone 813.5837
Director: Brigitta Jung-Nickel.
Contemporary international art non-aligned.
Open Monday-Friday 3-6, Saturday 10-1.
Underground: Krumme Lanke.

Galerie Krakowianka

Europa-Centre, 1000 Berlin 30, Telephone 262.4321
Director: Mr Juhr
Exhibitions of Polish art.
Open Monday-Friday 10-6, Saturday 10-2.
Underground: Zoologische Garten.

Galerie Kreutzmann

Windscheidstraße 18, 1000 Berlin 12, Telephone 323.6004
Artists' studios showing painting and installations. Other work including work by international artists also exhibited. Led by Gerd Kreutzmann
Open Monday-Friday 10-6, Saturday 3-6
Underground: Wilmersdorfer Straße

Kunst & Beton

Mommsenstraße 21, 1000 Berlin 12, Telephone 324 1591
Director: Bernd Berger
Gallery and studio showing only sculpture, mainly by sculptors living in Berlin, including Fehrenbach, Klaus Müller-Klug and Schmettau.
Examples of house facade ornamentation, of particular interest with current rebuilding in Berlin, are also sometimes on show.
Open Tuesday-Friday 2-7, Saturday 11-3
Underground: Adenauer Platz

Galerie im Kutscherhaus

Tempelhofer Ufer 11, 1000 Berlin 61, Telephone 251.7247/791.8359
Director: Hans Stober
Mr Stober has opened a gallery in this wonderful old coachman's house to display contemporary art. Works shown in alternating exhibitions are for sale but the gallery itself is non-commercial. One can often see works not often displayed elsewhere in West Berlin.
Open Monday-Friday 2-5
Underground: Möckernbrücke

Galerie Lietzow

Knesebeckstraße 32, 1000 Berlin 12, Telephone 881 2895
Director: Karl-Horst Hartmann.
An established important gallery with elegance and flair. Though not fixed to a particular 'school' figurative art is prominent. The line-up of artists is international; Ackermann, Amat, Caballero, Elsner, Marwan, Merz, Schenkel, Schmettau, Schoenholtz.
Open Tuesday-Friday 10-1 and 3-6, Saturday 10-2
Underground: Uhlandstraße

Galerie Lothar Sperlich

Blissesstraße 54, 1000 Berlin 31, Telephone 882.6180
Director: Lothar Sperlich

International graphics from 1600 to contemporary with concentration on works from the end of the nineteenth century until 1950. Traditional. Also sells for collections.
Open Monday-Friday 4-7.30, Saturday 10-2
Underground: Blissestraße/Bundesplatz/Heidelbergerplatz

Galerie Ludwig Lange

Wielandstraße 26 1000 Berlin 15, Telephone 881.2926
Director: Ludwig Lange
One of the few galleries in West Berlin specialising in sculpture with particular concentration on nineteenth and twentieth century bronze sculpture and sculpture realising form created out of the material. Emphasis on the 'Berlin School' from Schadow to Schoenholtz, the traditional contemporary, both figurative and abstract.
Open Tuesday-Friday 11-6, Saturday 10-2
Underground: Adenauer Platz

Galerie Marina Dinkler

Niebuhrstraße 77, 1000 Berlin 12, Telephone 881 9677
Director: Marina Dinkler
Marina Dinkler's special interest is contemporary Japanese art and the art created from the meeting of Eastern and Western traditions. Artists include Shoichi Ida, Kunito Nagaoka, Tetsuya Node.
Open Tuesday-Saturday 12-6
Underground: Kurfürstendamm/Witternbergplatz, then bus 19/29

Galerie Michael Haas

Niebuhrstraße 5, 1000 Berlin 12, Telephone 882.7006
Director: Michael Haas
Specialises in twentieth century painting, from the classical moderns such as Beckmann and Grosz, to contemporaries such as Chia and Clemente
Open Monday-Friday 3-6.30, Saturday 11-2
Underground: Adenauer Platz

Galerie Milan

Pfalzburger Straße 76, 1000 Berlin 15, Telephone 882 2803
Director: Milan Nesić
Concentration on contemporary figurative painting and a special interest in contemporary Yugoslavian art.
Open Monday-Thursday 4-7
Underground: Spichernstraße/Hohenzollerndamm

Galerie Nalepa

Riehlstraße 14, 1000 Berlin 19, Telephone 321.6845
Director: Ms Nalepa
Contemporary painting and sculpture. Artists include Miguel Esteben Cano, Albrecht Demitz, Titus.
Open Monday-Saturday 2-8

Underground: Kaiserdamm

Galerie Niebuhr

Kanstrße 142 1000 Berlin 12, Telephone 312.8763
Director: Herr Niebuhr
Gallery specialising in naive painting.
Open Tuesday-Friday 4.30-6.30, Saturday 11-2
Underground: Wilmersdorfer Straße

Galerie November

Bleibtreustraße 7, 1000 Berlin 12, Telephone 313. 7500
Director: Ulrike Turin
International contemporary 'phantastische realismus'. Exhibitions of artist-director Turin: also Escher, Mordstein, Müllerstaedt, Schmeisser.
Open Tuesday, Wednesday, Friday 4-6, Saturday 11-2
Underground: Kurfürstendamm/S-Bahn Savigny Platz

Galerie Oberlicht

Wartenburgstraße 17, 1000 Berlin 61, Telephone 785.9383
Director: Barbara Kuschnerus.
A gallery showing traditional modern realistic paintings, drawings and sculpture.
Open Wednesday 5-8, Saturday 12-5.
Underground: Möckernbrücke.

Galerie Oscar Davidson

Bleibtreustraße 48, 1000 Berlin 12, Telephone 883.3762
Director: Oscar Davidson.
Mainly German and French art, 1925 to contemporary. Annual exhibition by Russian artist/s.
Open Monday-Friday 2-6.30, Saturday 11-2
Underground: Kurfürstendamm

Galerie Pels-Leusden

Kurfürstendamm 58, 1000 Berlin 15, Telephone 323.5048/323.2044
Director: Hans Pels-Leusden. Partner Bernd Schulz.
Alternating exhibitions of German classical and modern art; Impressionists and Expressionists. Some exhibitions thematic. Artists include: Corinth, Heckel, Kollwitz, Macke, Marc. Some contemporary works. Also a fine graphics' collection. (Note the bookshop — see also literature section).
Open Monday-Friday 10-6.30, Saturday 10-2.
Underground: Adenauer Platz

Galerie Pfeiffenberger

Pfuelstraße 5, 1000 Berlin 36, Telephone 612.3030
Director: Katherina Pfeiffenberger
Contemporary international painting, interest in abstractionism. Artists include Gernot Bubenik, Ouhi Cha, Manfred Henkel.

Opening at Gallery Poll

Open Tuesday-Friday 11-1 and 2-7, Saturday and Sunday 3-7
Underground: Schlesisches Tor.

Galerie Pohlmann

Knesebeckstraße 17, 1000 Berlin 12, Telephone 312.1211
Director: Mr Pohlmann
Gallery situated near the Hochschule der Künste showing works
by art students studying there.
Open Monday-Friday 3-6
Underground: Ernst-Reuter-Platz

Galerie Pommersfeld

Knesebeckstraße 97, 1000 Berlin 12, Telephone 313 8005
Director: Mr Meyker
Small gallery with no fixed direction but concentration on interna-
tional painting of the 1920's and 1930's as well as contemporary
art.
Open Tuesday-Friday 12-6, by appointment in weekends.
Underground: Ernst-Reuter-Platz

Galerie Poll

Lützoplatz 7, 1000 Berlin 30, Telephone 261.7091
Director: Eva Poll
When Critical Realism (also known as Ugly Realism) was at its
peak, Galerie Poll was *the* gallery showing it. Eva Poll now concentrates on contemporary figurative and, in particular, the ex-
pressive tendency in German painting. In this way Galerie Poll
has provided a direct line from the group 'Großgörschen 35' to
their pupils Chevalier, Gabriel, Kaps, who are now exhibited there.
Sculpture is also a feature — the gallery's space and light lending
itself well to exhibitions of, for example, Goertz or Schmettau.

Open Monday 10-1, Tuesday-Friday 11-1, and 4-7, Saturday 11-3.
Underground: Nollendorfplatz

POLLstudio SO 36

Köpenicker Straße 194, 1000 Berlin 36, Telephone 261.7091
Eva Poll has also opened a smaller gallery in Kreuzberg mainly
showing photography and works by young artists. Exhibitions are
not regular; it is therefore best to phone before visiting to make an
appointment.
Underground: Schlesisches Tor.

Galerie Rampoldt

Giesebrechtstraße 13, 1000 Berlin 12, Telephone 883.3162
Director: Mr Rampoldt
The tendency of this gallery is more towards the figurative, but it
not tied to this. Mainly painting, at times sculpture. Artists in-
clude: Jiří Anderele, Quim Curuminas, Jochen Peeck, Christian
Rickert, Georg Seibert and Klaus Vogelgesang
Open Tuesday-Friday 4-8, Saturday 11-3
Underground: Adenauer Platz

Galerie Ritscher & Sandmeier

Reichstraße 104/11, 1000 Berlin 19, Telephone 301.5047/803.1452
Director: Alexander Sandmeier.
Mainly contemporary German painting.
By appointment only
Underground: Theodor-Heuss-Platz

Galerie Schüler

Kurfürstendamm 51, 1000 Berlin 15, Telephone 881.6361.
Director: Walter Schüler
Mr Schüler opened his gallery about 40 years ago in his Zehlen-
dorf apartment and exhibited German Expressionists. Later, he
became well-known for showing the abstract expressionists, for
example, Winter, Trier, Schütze, Thieler. He now shows both
realistic and abstract painting — an unconventional mixture for
Berlin, and some sculpture.
Open Tuesday-Friday 3-6, Saturday 10-2
Underground: Uhlandstraße

Galerie Springer

Fasanenstraße 13, 1000 Berlin 12. Telephone 313 9088
Director: Rudolf Springer
Springer is the best known art dealer in West Berlin and during his
36 year involvement with contemporary art he has become, as has
his gallery, something of an institution. Already in the 60's he was
showing Baselitz, he 'discovered' Bellmer, Calder and Lüpertz,
was the first gallery in Germany to show Miro (1950), held the first
Berlin exhibitions (1954) of Max Ernst and Nay, brought to Berlin
Léger, Mondrian and Picasso and today offers Armando, Baselitz,
Dichgans, Dorazio, Hödicke, Immendorf, Kirkeby, Lüpertz, Penck,

to name some. . . Springer simply chooses what he likes!
Open Tuesday-Friday 2-7, Saturday 11-2
Underground: Kurfürstendamm

Galerie Sylvie Menzel

Knesebeckstraße 20-21, 1000 Berlin 12, Telephone 310.850.
Director: Sylvia Menzel
International contemporary painting and sometimes drawing.
Main artists: Beuys, Chia, Fetting, Hödicke, Warhol. Also limited
editions of signed posters, for example by Hockney and Matisse.
Open Tuesday-Friday 2-6.30, Saturday 10-2
Underground: Ernst-Reuter-Platz

Gallery Nierendorf

Hardenbergstraße 19, 1000 Berlin 12, Telephone 785.6060
Director: Florian Karsch.
The oldest modern gallery in West Berlin, founded in 1920, closed
by the Nazis in 1936, rebuilt by Florian Karsch and family during
the last 30 years. The founder, Karl Nierendorf, was one of the
first to recognise and encourage the 'new', as they were in the
1920's and 30's: Beckmann, Braque, Dix, Feininger, Grosz,
Heckel, Kandinsky, Klee, Kirchner, Kokoschka, Marc, Mueller,
Nolde, Picasso. . . and the gallery today continutes the feast,
covering mainly the years 1905-1935 in Germany. A gallery important both for its history and its quality.
Open Monday-Friday 2-6, Saturday 10-2
Underground: Zoologische Garten

Galerie Redmann

Fasanenstraße 30, 1000 Berlin 15, Telephone 881.1135
Director: Mr. Redmann

Salome, a New Fauve painter

No particular emphasis. Many American artists, especially from the North West, are shown. Generally exhibitions of international classical modern and contemporary art. Artists include: James G. Davis, Jack Dollhausen, Scott Fife, Robert Helm, Gerd Marschand and Pavlos.
Open Tuesday-Friday 11-6, Saturday 11-2
Underground: Kurfürstendamm

Galerie am Savignyplatz

Carmerstraße 10, 1000 Berlin 12, Telephone 313.6564
Director: Dr Friedrich Rothe
Mainly traditional, realistic oils and water-colours. (Dr. Rothe is only interested in artists over 30).
Open Tuesday-Friday 3-7, Saturday 11-2
Underground: Ernst-Reuter-Platz

Galerie Taube

Pariser Straße 54, 1000 Berlin 15, Telephone 883.5694
Director: Klaus Märtens
Emphasis on twentieth century figurative art and especially forgotten artists. Artists include: Dickman, Francke, Lesser, Mantovani, Otto, Schoff, Torrilhon, Willig. Sometimes photography.
Open Tuesday-Friday 4-7, Saturday 11-2
Underground: Spichernstraße

Galerie Westphal

Fasanenstraße 68, 1000 Berlin 15, Telephone 882.1162
Director: Volker Westphal
Nineteenth and twentieth century art with emphasis on French painting of this century and Berlin art.
Open Monday-Friday 10-1, and 2-6.30, Saturday 10-2
Underground: Uhlandstraße

Paintings by Johannes Grutzke at the Laden galerie

Galerie 2000

Knesebeckstraße 56/58, 1000 Berlin 15, Telephone 883.8467
Director: Wolfgang Chrobok
The gallery is the twin of the Knesebeckstraße art bookshop. Six
exhibitions each year: concentration on realists. Artists include
Horst Janssen, Rainer Kriester, Fritz Köthe
Open Monday-Friday 9.30-6.30, Saturday 9.30-2
Underground: Uhlandstraße

Haus am Lützowplatz

Lützowplatz 9, 1000 Berlin 30, Telephone 261.3805
The gallery is run by an art association and shows contemporary
art, mainly representational, documents about Berlin history and
caricature.
Open Tuesday-Sunday 11-6
Underground: Nollendorfplatz

Kuhdamm Galerie

Kurfürstendamm 61, 1000 Berlin 15, Telephone 882.6761
Director: Mr Kornbichler
Twentieth century painting. Artists include Gerhard Andrés,
Albrecht Demitz, Helga Ginerwa
Open Monday-Friday 10-8, Saturday 10-2
Underground: Adenauer Platz

Ladengalerie

Kurfürstendamm 64, 1000 Berlin 15, Telephone 881.4214
Director: Karoline Müller
A renowned West Berlin gallery concentrating on contemporary,
mainly German relists. Art from the German Democratic Republic
and Poland as well.
Open Monday-Friday 10-6.30, Saturday 10-2, 10-6 on the first
Saturday of each month.
Underground: Adenauer Platz

Majakowski Galerie

Kurfürstendamm 72, 1000 Berlin 31, Telephone 323.3076/241.935
Specialises in twentieth century Soviet and East German pain-
ting, graphics and sculpture and West Berlin art.
Open Tuesday-Friday 2-5 or by appointment.
Underground: Adenauer Platz

Off Galerie

Joachim-Friedrich-Straße 34, 1000 Berlin 31, Telephone 891.5873
Director: Ms Bahlsen
Young and established artists; among the latter Camaro and
Heiliger
Open Tuesday-Friday 3-6, Saturday 12-2
Underground: Adenauer Platz

Ouroborus

Stephanstraße 26, 1000 Berlin 21, Telephone 396 3025
Director: Thea Fischer-Reinhardt
International contemporary art.
Open Tuesday-Friday 3-6.30, 11-2.
Underground: Birkenstraße

Petersen Galerie

Pestalozzistraße 106, 1000 Berlin 12, Telephone 313 4508/8237395
Director: Jes Petersen
A gallery for the extraordinary and the avant garde. Artists include: Barfuß, Brus, Gosewitz, Nitsch, Roth, Wachweger
Open Monday-Friday 3-7, Saturday 11-2
Underground: Ernst-Reuter-Platz

Pola Arto-J.S. Skorupski

Dorfstraße 57b, 1000 Berlin 20, Telephone 331.6688
Director: Mr Skorupski
Contemporary painting, sculpture and graphics by young and well-known Polish artists.
By appointment only
Underground: Ruhleben, then all buses in direction Spandau.

Raab Galerie

Potsdamer Straße 58, 1000 Berlin 30, Telephone 261.6098
Director: Ingrid Raab
Specialises in contemporary Berlin art; neo-expressionism. One of the first galleries to concentrate on the formerly known 'Moritz-boys', now the famous 'Wilden'. Major artists exhibited are: Bach,

Ingrid Raab, gallery owner. Salome painting in the background

Chevalier, Fetting, Salomé, Schindler
Open Monday-Friday 11-6.30, Saturday 10-2
Underground: Kurfürstenstraße, then bus 29 to the Nationalgalerie stop. Also buses 83 and 48

Reinhard Onnasch Galerie

Fasanenstraße 47, 1000 Berlin 15, Telephone 882.7718
Director: Reinhard Onnasch.
Two main directions are shown by this gallery, international classical art of the '60's and young German artists. Among the artists: Adamski, Bömmels, Flavin, Kienholz, Koberling, Matta, Deehlen, Siegel.
Open Monday-Friday 3-6.30, Saturday 11-2
Underground: Kurfürstendamm

Scanart

Fasanenstraße 41, 1000 Berlin 15, Telephone 882.3528
Director: Ishild Schauseit
A relatively new gallery, opened in September 1984, showing contemporary Scandinavian art; oils, water-colours, sculpture and an annual graphics exhibition. Among the main artists: Aschenbrenner, Cullberg, Magnus, Pettersen, Reumert.
Open Tuesday-Friday 3-7, Saturday 11-2
Underground: Spichernstraße

Sonne Berlin

Kanstraße 138, 1000 Berlin 12, Telephone 312.2355
Director: Christian Holzfuß and Klaus Sonne
Mainly abstract painting by young international and German artists including: Katja Hajek, Joachim F. Kettel, Barbara Quandt
Open Tuesday-Friday 3-6, Saturday 1-4
Underground: Zoologische Garten, then bus 92/SBahn Savigny Platz

Scanart gallery, Fasanenstrasse which specialises in Scandinavian art

Tipheret—Stätte der Schönen Künste

Detmolder Straße 2, 1000 Berlin 31, Telephone 853.9664/851.1247
Director: Mr and Ms Dietzmann
New gallery, includes work with Jewish or Israeli themes.
Open Monday-Thursday 4-7, Friday 4-6.
Underground: Bundesplatz

Weekend Gallery/Foreign Office

Scholßstraße 62 1000 Berlin 19, Telephone 342.9287/341.4157
Run by a collective, with the aim of encouraging young artists.
Opening times change according to the exhibition, best to phone
first.
Underground: Sophie-Charlotte-Platz

Wewerka Gallery

Fasanenstraße 41a, 1000 Berlin 15, Telephone 882.6739
Fritschestraße 27/28, 1000 Berlin 10.
Director: Michael Wewerka
In the long term the Fasanenstraße address is the more impor-
tant. The Fritschestraße gallery is a large loft where the space
allows action painting or performance. Apart from the difference
in size determining choice of exhibition neither gallery is limited
to a direction although abstract painting is important to both. Ar-
tists include: Heinig, Lixfeld, Ono, Schling, Vostell.
Fasanenstraße open Tuesday-Friday 2.30-6.30, Saturday 10-2
Fritchestraße best to telephone.
Underground: for Fasanenstraße: Spichernstraße
Underground: for Frichestraße: Sophie-Charlotte-Platz

Zellermayer Gallerie

Ludwigkirchstraße 14, 1000 Berlin 15, Telehone
883.4144/831.1797.
Director: Carsta Zellermayer
Experimental; was the first gallery in West Germany to exhibit
Swiss artist Urs Lüthi, the sculptor Erwin Wurm and to show Bar-
bara Heinisch's action painting. Zellermayer artists include:
Höckelmann, Hacker, Lange, Meldner, Wiegand and Czech col-
lagist Jiri Kolar
Open Tuesday-Friday 3-6.30, Saturday 11-2.
Underground: Spichernstraße

Selbsthilfgalerien
(Self-help galleries)

It is important to note that the list of selbsthilfgalerien (literally
translated as self-help galleries) is a constantly changing one and
that the members of such galleries and their addresses and
telephone numbers also change frequently.
   Already since right after the Second World War
selbsthilfgalerien were a traditional part of Berlin's artistic life.
The typical selbsthilfgalerie — if one can so generalise — is
created by a group of young artists, usually in their 20's, who col-

lectively rent a studio or rooms to show their works, either individually or collectively. The costs and the profits are shared equally. Sometimes the space rented also serves as a studio, or even living quarters. There are also 'single' selbsthilfgalerien, where an artist will exhibit his or her work in a studio.

Three to four years is the average time a selbsthilfgalerie will stay open, though there are often changes in membership and exhibitions are usually irregular. For young artists the concept is not only of financial benefit but a chance to exhibit and, perhaps above all, a learning process whereby each can enjoy the critical appraisal, support and inspiration of the rest of the group. What's more, though most such galleries die a natural death some are the beginnings of later fame in the international art world — as the 'Junge Wilden' have demonstrated.

Atelier ad absurdum

Friesenstraße 25, 1000 Berlin 61, Telephone 692.1452
Selbsthilfgalerie of Rolf Burkart
Graphics, drawings, offset and hand-printing
By appointment
Underground: Gneisernaustraße

Atelier JA

Hildegardstraße 21a, 1000 Berlin 31, Telephone 853.7831
Selbsthilfgalerie of young artists. Sometimes exhibitions in the context of social themes. Crafts also.
Open Tuesday-Friday 5-7.30, and by appointment
Underground: Blissestraße, then bus 86, three stops in direction Steglitz.

Aufbau-Abbau

Oranienstraße 47a, 1000 Berlin 61, Telephone 653.115
This is the studio of partners Heika Kempken and Rainald Schumacher where they show their own work and also that of young international atists. Painting and sculpture.
Daily 3-9
Underground: Mortizplatz

Der Standort

Kolonnenstraße 26, 1000 Berlin 62, Telephone 781.5238/654.432/614.8618
Selbsthilfgalerie of Boris Doempke, Susanne Mahlmeister, Hannes Forster.
Installations. The group also exhibit in West Germany and internationally.
Best to telephone first for exhibition times as they change.
Underground: Mortizplatz, bus 20 to Oranienplatz

Dreigroschengalerie

Mariannenplatz 23, Floor 2, 1000 Berlin 36, Telephone 611.5733
Collective of four Berlin women artists: Roswitha Jakiza, Marina

Wolfgang Petrick, the Critical Realist

Maliniki, Renata Richter, Ricarda Tatzke. Critical, politcally conscious art, but not propaganda. Five exhibitions or so each year; sometimes by guests.
Open Friday 8-10pm, Saturday 5-9pm, Sunday 3-6pm
Underground: Kottbusser Tor

Droysen-Galerie

Droysen Straße 17, 1000 Berlin 12, Telephone 324.6919.
Collective of three, contact Sybille Windt
Mainly paintings, sometimes sculpture, by young Berlin artists, usually Hochschule der Künste students. Not interested in the purely abstract, nor the purely naturalistic, more what lies between.
Open Thursday and Friday 3-7, Saturday 11-2
Underground: Adenauer Platz

endart

Oranienstraße 36, Kreuzberg
Artists' collective of Sir Ralph/Anus, Chicken/Jim Pansen, Klar Bier/Tom China, Ignaz/Gerd Rouge/Kermet Krebs/Heiner Kuttel, Klara Korn/Mae Bowle/Dolores Käferli
'Off-Off' painting, sculpture, reliefs, performance, music, comics, photography — sometimes called Crossculture. The name 'endart' signals the grops belief that established art definitions, indeed established art forms, should and well end, so no description will be entertained here.
Open for your pleasure and opinion.
Underground: Moritzplatz

Galerie Atelier Nil

Rostocker Straße 3, 1000 Berlin 21, Telephone 391.3654

Studio and exhibition space of Neil Ausländer. Interested in 'The human being in our time'. Also believes art prices are too high!
Open daily 6-8
Underground: Turmstraße

Galerie Henz

Ebersstraße 12, 1000 Berlin 62, Telephone 784.1435
Selbsthilfgalerie of 'master pupils' of Hochschule der Künste.
Open Wednesday and Friday 4-8, Saturday and Sunday 12-4.
Underground: Kleistpark

Galerie ix Atelier

Kyffhäuserstraße 24, 1000 Berlin 30, Telephone 215.2278/786.6189
Studio and gallery of Inge Husemann
Open Tuesday and Thursday 3-7, Saturday 11-5 or by appointment
Underground: Nollendorfplatz

Galerie Gras Fressen

Muthesiusstraße 15, 1000 Berlin 41, Telephone 344.8244
Collective selbsthilfgalerie shared by Susannah Knaack, Martin von Oftteovski, Paul Refllio, Michaela Seliger, Petra Varmka, H.H. Zvanzig. Usually thematic exhibitions.
Open Thursday-Sunday 4-7
Underground: Schloßstraße

Galerie No Name

Sybelstraße 38, 1000 Berlin 12, Telephone 324.3495
The selbsthilfgalerie of artist No Name. Often works in the context of socio-political themes. Exhibitions also by other artists.
Open Tuesday-Friday 4-7 during exhibitions, otherwise by appointment.
Underground: Adenauer Platz

Galerie Pegasus

Emser Straße 45, 1000 Berlin 15, Telephone 881.6512
Director: Frau Kunze and Peter Feinauer
This was the first gallery in West Germany to show Copy Art and is especially interested in colour Copy Art. Exhibitions also of painting and sculpture, audio art and audio clothing.
Open Monday-Friday 3-6.30, Saturday 11-2.
Underground: Hohenzollerndam

Galerie '6 in 36'

Oranienstraße 9, 1000 Berlin 36, Telephone 612.5478
Selbsthilfgalerie of students of Hödicke, more abstract however.
Open Friday, Saturday and Sunday 5-7.30
Underground: Gürlitzer Bahnhof.

Galerie Verein Berliner Künstler

Schöneberger Ufer 57, 1000 Berlin 30, Telephone 261.2399
Director: Mr Mordelt
Non-commercial gallery showing works by the 70 or so member
artists, and guests; interested in all directions and mediums ex-
cept crafts. Holds archives.
Open daily, except Monday, 1-6, Sunday 1-5.
Underground: Kurfürstenstraße, bus 29.

Galerie Wissarth

Pfuehlstraße 5, 1000 Berlin 36, Telephone 611.5823
Selbsthilfgalerie of five artists: Eva Gröttum, Liv Mette Larsen,
Roza Spak, Herbert Wiegand, Yana Yo. Each artist works in a dif-
ferent direction. Other artists are also exhibited. Interest in the br-
inging together of the arts; painting, sculpture, film, performance,
music, video.
By appointment
Underground: Schlesisches Tor.

Garage

Crellestraße 16, 1000 Berlin 62, Telephone
791.8359/784.8667/623.7999
An important, active selbsthilfgalerie existing now for four years.
Collective formed by painters V. Jo Bruner, Jürgen Frisch, Petra
Seelenmeyer and Dirk Sommer
Open Saturday and Sunday 1-6
Underground: Kleistpark

Institut Unzeit

Erkelenzdamm 11-13, B1V, 1000 Berlin 36, Telephone 652.702.
A loft used collectively by painters and sculptors and for perfor-
mances of experimental music organised by the Freunde Guter
Musik Berlin (see also music section)
Underground: Kottbusser Tor.

K.19

Klausenerplatz 19, 1000 Berlin 19, Telephone 322.2060
An important selbsthilfgalerie, run as a collection. Studio and ex-
hibition space, also at times other art forms, for example theatre.
Telephone first to make an appointment
Underground: Sophie-Charlotte-Platz

Lot Quartier

Rheistraße 45, Innenhof, aufg 3, IV, Telephone 851.2059
Collective founded in 1979, members are Louis Engeln, Gabriele
Fox, Wolfgang Heder, Wendelin Hinsch, Christian Rickert and
Arulf Spengler. The artists sometimes exhibit together, other
times individually. Their styles are experimental, each different,
all however motivated by a special interest in the materials and
processes used and spatial relationsips. Sometimes other artists

are invited to exhibit
During exhibitions, open Wednesday and Friday 3-6, Saturday 11-2, but best to phone first.
Underground: Walter-Schreiber-Platz

Neupertinger Kabinett

Saarstraße 9, 1000 Berlin 41, Telephone 852.1023
Formerly a gallery and artist's studio. Not a conventional gallery, but a place for viewing although one can buy. Specialises in 'ceramic monsters', each with a story attached, a traditional art from Southern Germany
Open Monday, Tuesday 11-1 and 3-6, also by appointment.
Underground: Friedrich-Wilhelm-Platz

Qual der Wahl Galerie

Reichenberger Straße 29, 1000 Berlin 36, Telephone 612.4448
Exhibitions in the studio of Dutch artist H.L. Booy.
Telephone to check times.
Underground: Kottbusser Tor.

Quergalerie

Wriezener Straße 35, 1000 Berlin 65, Telephone 494.4265/493.7289
One of the most important selbsthilfgalerien in West Berlin, existing now for four years. Housed in a former factory with room for seven studios. Four artists also live in the building. The artists, though a collective, are not a homogeneous group and they produce a wide variety of different works; paintings, installations, sculpture, as well as holding concerts and performance. Non-commercial and 'Off'.
Open Thursday-Sunday 4-7.
Underground: Osloer Straße

Tupolew 144

Fichtstraße 31, 1000 Berlin 61
'Fringe' selbsthilfgalerie
Open Thursday-Sunday 5-7pm

Unart

Oranienstraße
'Underground' selbsthilfgalerie; performance, theatre, fashion as well as a gallery.
Underground: Kochstraße/Mortizplatz

Van Roy's Offenes Atelier

Holbeinstraße 11, 1000 Berlin 45, Telephone 833.2570
Individual and group exhibitions. Studio and exhibition space of sculptor Van Roy who exhibits his own work and that of others, also painters. Many directions but special interest in the artistic process itself — the beginning stages of Van Roy's work and their development ot the final work are shown together. Interest also in

works relating to their surroundings. Some exhibitions combine sculpture, painting and architecture.
Open Saturday and Sunday 4-8
Underground: Rathaus Steglitz, then bus 85 to Ringstraße, or S-Bahn Lichterfelde West, or Bus 11 to Holbein Straße

Galleries part of shops, restaurants etc.

Anderes Ufer

Haupstraße 157, 1000 Berlin, Telephone 784.1578
Director: Mr Hoffmann
Gallery and cafe combined. Shows young artists.
Open daily 11-2am
Underground: Kleistpark

Bücherbogen

Stadtbahnbogen 593 am Savignyplatz, 1000 Berlin 12, Telephone 312.1932. Art bookshop; different exhibitions relating to new books.
Open Monday-Friday 9.30-6.30, Saturday 10-2
Underground: Ernst-Reuter-Platz

Galerie Aue

Berliner Straße 48, 1000 Berlin 31, Telephone 874.978
Jazz pub with paintings displayed.
Open Monday-Friday 4-4am, Sunday 11-4pm
Underground: Berliner Straße

BHI Galerie Etage

Europa Center, Tauentzienstraße 9, 1000 Berlin 30.
Exhibitions in a bank
Open Monday-Wednesday 9-1, 2-3.15, Tuesday and Thursday 9-1, 3.30-6, Friday 9-1.
Underground: Zoologische Garten

Galerie Bernd E

Suaretzstraße 21, 1000 Berlin 19, Telephone 322.7792
Gallery behind shops for frames, contemporary German painters.
Open Tuesday-Friday 2-7.
Underground: Sophie-Charlotte-Platz

Galerie Carlos Hulsch

Emser Straße 43, 1000 Berlin 15, Telephone 882.2842
Director: Carlos Hulsch
Gallery and wine shp.
Open, usually, Tuesday-Friday 3-6.30/7.30, Saturday 11-2pm
Underground: Spichernstraße

Gerd Rohling with his exhibition at the artist owned Gallery 1/61 (1980)

Galerie Janssen

Pariser Straße 45, 1000 Berlin 15, Telephone 881 1590
Director: Volker Janssen
Exhibitions only about 'men in art'. Posters, postcards, books and magazines about men.
Open Monday-Friday 12-6.30, Saturday 11-2
Underground: Hohenzollernplatz

Galerie P'37

Pariser Straße 37, 1000 Berlin 15, Telephone 883.8262
Director: Mr Pintsch
Gallery with a children's shop. Shows contemporary international artists.
Open Monday-Friday 10-6, Saturday 10-2
Underground: Adenauer Platz

Galerie Ramdhanu

Goethestraße 78, 1000 Berlin 12, Telephone 312.1632
Director: Mr Ghosh and Mr Steadtler
Gallery alongside a shop which mainly sells Indian wares. The gallery is however open in direction and also, at times, shows crafts.
Open Monday-Friday 9.30-6.30, Saturday 9-2
Underground: Ernst-Reuter-Platz

Galerie im Steigenberger

Los Angeles Platz 1, 1000 Berlin 30, Telephone 210.8844
Gallery in Hotel Steigenberger; modern art.
Open 9am-10pm
Underground: Zoologische Garten

Galerie Terzo

Grolmanstraße 28, 1000 Berlin 12. Telephone 881.5261

Gallery in cafe
Open Tuesday-Sunday 12-2am
Underground: Ernst-Reuter-Platz/Kurfürstendamm

Gelbe Musik

Schaperstraße 11, 1000 Berlin 15, Telephone 211.3962
Director: Ursula Block
This record-shop specialising in avant-garde music (see music
section) at times also combines as a gallery and exhibits art
works exploring the relation between seeing and hearing —
hence the name Gelbe Musik or Yellow Music.
Open Monday-Friday 11-6, Saturday 11-1.
Underground: Spichernstraße

Gropiusche Buch-und Kunsthandlung

Hohenzollerndamm 170, 1000 Berlin 31, Telephone 860.00340
Director: Mr Pump
Regular exhibitions in bookshop; contemporary naturalistic pain-
ting; graphics and sculpture.
Open Monday-Friday 8.30-6.30, Saturday 9-1.
Underground: Fehrbelliner Platz

HS-Galerie

Bismarckstraße 84, 1000 Berlin 12, Telephone 313.8024
Director: Mr Seiffert
Gallery in a shop selling medical supplies.
Open Monday-Friday 10-6
Underground: Bismarckstraße

Kassandra Frauengalerie

Suarezstraße 41, 1000 Berlin 19, Telephone 321.2137
Director: Ms Finger
Only women artist's works accepted but interested in all media.
The gallery combines with a travel bureau and publishers and ex-
hibitions are therefore irregular. Best to phone first.
Open Monday-Friday 9-6, Saturday 12-2.
Underground: Sophie-Charlotte-Platz

Kleine Weltlaterne

Nestorstraße 22, 1000 Berlin 31, Telephone 892.6585
Formerly an important gallery, now combines with a restaurant.
Open daily 8pm-3am
Underground: Fehrbelliner Platz, then Bus 4 direction Roseneck.

Magasin Provencal

Seelingstraße 57, 1000 Berlin 19, Telephone 322.5950
Director: Richard Pettit
Gallery and wine shop. Contemporary art.
Open Monday-Friday 2-6.30, Saturday 10 to 2;
Underground: Sophie-Charlotte-Platz, Bus 74.

Fred Thieler, one of Germany's foremost abstract painters, a teacher at the Berlin Academy

Mora

Großbeerenstraße 57a, 1000 Berlin 61, Telephone 785.0585
Director: Mr Gieszle
Gallery and cafe
Open daily 10-midnight
Underground: Mehringdamm

Stodieck's Buchhandlung und Galerie

Richard-Wagner Straße 39, 1000 Berlin 10, Telephone 341.1040
Director: Mr Stodieck
Small gallery behind bookshop. Contemporary art, sometimes Polish artists.
Open Monday-Friday 9-18.30, Saturday 10-2
Underground: Richard-Wagner-Platz

GALLERIES IN INSTITUTIONS

Berliner Festspiele Galerie

Budapester Straße 48, 1000 Berlin 30, Telephone 254 890
Variety of exhibitions, best to telephone as exhibitions are not held regularly
Underground: Zoologische Garten

Centre Francais de Wedding

Müllerstraße 74, 1000 Berlin 65, Telephone 418.1418/418.1766
Varied exhibitions, mainly by French artists. The centre also shows films (French and German) and offers a programme of concerts, theatre and Chansson evenings. Exhibition viewing time, daily 10am-7pm. For other programme details see 'Tip' or 'Zitty' or

the Centre's published programme.
Underground: Rehberge

DIN—Galerie

in Haus der Norming (equivalent to the British Standards Institute) Burggrafenstraße 4-10, 1000 Berlin 30, Telephone 260.1333
A non-commercial gallery, though exhibits are for sale. The gallery shows work by artists living in Berlin (not necessarily Berlin born)
Open Monday-Friday 9-6.
Underground: Wittenbergplatz

Galerie im Deutschlandhaus

Stresemannstraße 90, 1000 Berlin 61, Telephone 261.1046
Director: Dr Wolfgang Schulz
Gallery showing variety of different exhibitions by artists born in, or connected with, East Germany.
Open Monday-Friday 10-6, Saturday 2-6
Studio gallery showing painting open Monday-Friday 9-7, Saturday and Sunday 2-7.
Underground: Möckernbrücke

Galerie im Fontanehouse

Wilhelmsruher Damm 142c, 1000 Berlin 26, Telephone 419.22151
The gallery exhibits contemporary German painting. Fontanehouse is a cultural centre with a library, club-rooms, cafe and holds evening classes, organises literary readings, concerts and theatre.
Open Monday-Friday 10am-9pm, Sunday 10am-1pm.

Galerie Transit im Kulturhaus

Breitenstraße 71a, 1000 Berlin 20, Telephone 333.5026
Shows work by young artists, not established.
Open Monday-Friday 3pm-6pm, Saturday 11am-3pm
Underground: Rathaus Spandau.

Galerie et Vins du Languedoc

Monumentenstraße 5, 1000 Berlin 62, Telephone 782.1522
Director: Nor C. Wilde
Gallery shows mainly contemporary Berlin art, sometimes also French artists. Private gallery, where the director works in conjunction with the French Government and sells products from Southern France.
Open Monday-Friday 3-8
Underground: Kleistpark

Goethe Institut

Knesebeckstraße 3-48, 1000 Berlin 15, Telephone 881.3052
Irregular exhibitions, best to phone first. Exhibitions usually by international artists.

One man show Karol Broniatowski at the Deplana Kunsthalle

During exhibitions, open Monday-Friday 9am-8pm, Wednesday 9am-6pm.
Underground: Uhlandstraße

Max-Planck-Institut für Bildungsforschung

Lentzealle 94, 1000 Berlin 33, Telephone 829.95308/9.
Exhibit mainly young Berlin artists.
Open Monday-Friday 8am-7pm, Saturday 8-1pm
Underground: Breitenbachplatz

Matthäus-Kirche an der Philharmonie

Matthäikirchplatz, 1000 Berlin 30, Telephone 261.3676
Exhibitions appropriate to the religious calendar or with religious themes and feelings. Four or five exhibitions each year.
Open for services, concerts and Thursday 2-6, Sunday 2-5
Underground: Kurfürstenstraße

Thelogisch-Pädagogische Akademie

Westendalles 54, 1000 Berlin 19. Telephone 305.1052
Director: Laurenz Ungruhe.
This is a Catholic Centre which also holds four exhibitions each year of art conveying religious themes.
Underground: Neu Westend

Werkbund Archiv

Scholßstraße 1, 1000 Berlin 19, Telephone 322.1061
Director: Mr Siepmann.
The Werkbund is an association existing since 1907 for architectural and design interests. The Archiv was founded in 1972 and organises exhibitions and publishes books and catalogues on ar-

chitecture and design. The exhibitions are often linked to historical contexts, for example, an exhibition of 1950's design. In one to two years the Werkbund-Archiv is planning to move to the Gropius-Bau.
Open Wednesday-Sunday 11-5, but best to phone first,
Underground: Richard-Wagner-Platz

PAINTINGS' LIBRARIES

Graphothek

Buddestraße 21, 1000 Berlin 27, Telephone 419.26212
A 'library' of paintings, that is, paintings lent out not sold.
Open Monday and Friday 3-8, Tuesday and Thursday 11-5.
Underground: Tegel.

Graphothek City

Heerstraße 12, 1000 Berlin 19.
Paintings, drawings, small sculptures lent out.
Open Monday-Friday 9-3, Thursday 9-6

SOME AUCTION HOUSES

Auktionshaus von Gerda Bassenge

Erdener Straße 5a, 1000 Berlin 33, Telephone 892.9013
Antique books and graphics.

Kunsthandel Leo Spik

Kurfürstendamm 65, 1000 Berlin 15, Telephone 883.6170
Painting

Kunsthandlung Reinhard Wolff

Lietzenburger Straße 92, 1000 Berlin 15, Telephone 882.2808
Seventeenth to nineteenth century works. Berlin graphics.

Note the combined annual exhibition in the Orangerie in Schloß Charlottenburg organised by the Verband Berliner Kunst und Antiquitätenhändler e.V. (Kurfürstendamm 58, 1000 Berlin 15, Telephone 323.2046)

PHOTOGRAPHY GALLERIES

Brennpunkt Galerie für Fotografie

Elberfelder Straße 13, 1000 Berlin 13, Berlin 21, Telephone 392.1665.
Open Wednesday-Friday 5-7pm, Saturday 11-2
Underground: Turmstraße

Fotodesign

Langenscheidtstraße 3, 1000 Berlin 62, Telephone 782.4635

Director: Frank Wolffram
Small photography gallery. Mainly contemporary.
Open Monday-Friday 9.30-1 and 2.30-6.30, Saturday 9.30-1
Underground: Kleistpark

Fotogalerie 70

Tempelhofer Ufer 22, 1000 Berlin Telephone 216.3043
Director: Mr Schröder
Contemporary photography, documents, posters, postcards, sometimes painting. Often thematic exhibitions. Interest in the 'alternative scene'.
Open Tuesday-Friday 12-7, Saturday and Sunday 2-5

Gerson Fehrenbach the sculptor in his studio

Fotogalerie im Wedding

Amsterdamer Straße 24, 1000 Berlin 65, Telephone 456.2918.
A collective. Only contemporary photography, mainly from West Germany.
Open Tuesday-Friday 2-7, Saturday 11-5.
Underground: Seestraße

Landesbildstelle Berlin

Wilkingerufer 7, 1000 Berlin 21, Telephone 390.921
Centre for audio-visual material. See also section on archives.
Open daily, except Wednesday from 9-3, and Thursday until 6 during the school year.
Underground: Hansa Platz.

Werkstatt für Photographie

Friedrichstraße 210, 1000 Berlin 61, Telephone 258 87866
Part of Volkshochschule Kreuzberg. Opened in 1976, the Werkstatt offers tuition in photography with an emphasis on photography as a means of individual artistic expression. The course is open to everyone. Exhibitions are also held in the Werkstatt's galleries and there are also regular workshops to which well-known German and international photographers are invited. To help finance the costs of exhibitions and workshops an association, the 'Freunde der Werkstatt für Photographie' was formed.
Open Monday-Friday 5-8.
Underground: Friedrichstraße

CRAFT GALLERIES

There are several excellent shops selling pottery in Berlin but no gallery devoted exclusively to pottery.

Die Werkstattgalerie

Meierottostraße 1, 1000 Berlin 15, Telephone 881.1896.
Director: Ms Brodhag and Ms Wörn
Three to four exhibitions each year of contemporary jewellery.
Open Monday-Friday 10-6, Saturday 10-2pm
Underground: Spichernstraßbe

Galerie in der Goldschmiede Nikolassee

Prinz-Friedrich-Leopold-Straße 5, 1000 Berlin 38, Telephone 803.4598/803.1452
Director: Helga Ritscher-Sandkuhl.
Gallery showing antique and new jewellery, generally 17th to 19th century inclusive, also contemporary English, French, German, Dutch, Italian, Spanish pieces. About three or four exhibitions each year.
Open Tuesday-Friday 10-1 and 3-6, Saturday 10-1
S-Bahn Nikolassee or buses 53 or 18.

Galerie des Lichts

Goethestraße 81, 1000 Berlin 12, Telephone 317.548
Director: Marlene Laser
Contemporary neon-light sculpture, photography, painting, glass,
pottery, sculpture. Mainly glass.
Open Tuesday-Friday 2-7, Saturday 11-2.
Underground: Ernst-Reuter-Platz

Galerie Kunsthandwerk Berlin E.v.

Pariser Straße 12, 1000 Berlin 15, Telephone 881.3862
Director: Sybille Voorman.
Gallery run by the Berlin handcraft association, showing a variety
of crafts.
Open Tuesday-Friday 12-6.30, Saturday 10-2.
Underground: Spichernstraße

Galerie Neiriz

Kurfürstendamm 175, 1000 Berlin 15, Telephone 882.3232
Director: Ms Pregley.
Large gallery showing nineteenth century textiles, new exhibition
every three months or so.
Open Monday-Friday 2-9pm, Saturday 11-1 or 10-6 on the first
Saturday of each month.
Underground: Adenauer Platz

Seibert-Philippen

Giesebrechtstraße 15, 1000 Berlin 12, Telephone 883.6446
Director: Ms Seibert-Philippen.
German and International contemporary jewellry. One or two ex-
hibitions each year.
Open Monday-Friday 10-6pm, Saturday and Sunday 10-2.
Underground: Adenauer Platz

Textilkunst-Galerie Rasmussen

Pariser Straße 40, 1000 Berlin 15, Telephone 882.1167.
Textiles' studio and gallery of Ute Bredov who mainly designs and
makes patchworks and Rolando Rasmussen who designs and
makes clothing. Modern, rather than traditional or folk. Approx-
imately two exhibitions per year.
Open Monday-Friday 11-1 and 3-7, Saturday 11-2.
Underground: Spichernstraße

Some Other Jewellery addresses:

Feinschmeide

Windscheidstraße 24, 1000 Berlin 12, Telephone 323.4048
Open Monday-Friday 11-6.30, Saturday 10-2;

Richter

Knesebeckstraße 27, 1000 Berlin 12, Telephone 881.2179.
Open weekdays, except Wednesday, 10-12 and 2-6.30, Saturday
10-1

Rodalquilar

Schlüterstraße 30, 1000 Berlin 12, Telephone 324.1991
Open Tuesday-Friday 12-6.30, Saturday 11-3.

KUNSTAMT GALLERIES

Galerie Franz Mehring

Mehringplatz 7, 1000 Berlin 61, Telephone 2588-1.
Gallery run by Kunstamt Kreuzberg, showing mainly Kreuzberg artists.
Open Wednesday-Sunday 3-7.
Underground: Hallesches Tor, (exit Friedrichstraße)

Galerie im Körnerpark

Schierker Straße 8, 1000 Berlin 44, Telephone 680.92431.
Director: Dr Kolland
Kunstamt gallery of Neukölln mainly showing contemporary German painting.
Open Tuesday-Sunday 11-5.
Underground: Neukölln

Haus am Kleistpark

Grundwaldstraße 6&7, 1000 Berlin 62, Telephone 783.3032.
Varying exhibitions, sometimes art but also other exhibitions, for
example about the area of Schöneberg. Best to phone first.
Exhibition times Tuesday-Sunday 2/3-7pm depending upon what
is shown.
Underground: Kleistpark.

Haus am Waldsee

Argentinische Allee 30, 1000 Berlin 37, Telephone
801.8935/807.2234
Director: Thomas Kempas
Zehlendorf has housed its art centre in a beautiful old villa surrounded by a park. Exhibitions in its gallery and a programme of
music dance and theatre.
Gallery open Tuesday-Sunday 10-6.
Underground: Krumme Lanke

Galerie in der Zitadelle

Straße am Juliusturm, 1000 Berlin 20, Telephone 330.32234
Kunstamt Spandau gallery showing a variety of exhibitions.
Open Tuesday-Friday 9-4, Saturday and Sunday 10-4.

Obere Galerie

Lützoplatz 9 (Haus am Lützoplatz), 1000 Berlin 30, Telephone 390.5234.
Gallery administered by Kunstamt Tiergarten, generally showing contemporary art.
Open Tuesday-Sunday 11-6
Underground: Nollerndorfplatz.

THE FINE ARTS — FINANCIAL HELP TO ARTISTS.

Unlike most Western cities West Berlin has no significant private institutionalised money invested in the fine arts. The Berlin Senate is therefore the centre for financial backing. The Senate supports directly and indirectly. An example of direct financial help is the Arbeitstipendium, or scholarship system, whereby every year ten artists each receive a scholarship worth around 10,000 DM (1984 figure). The artists are chosen by an independent jury. There are also schemes and scholarships to help artists work in other countries, for instance P.S.I. scholarships to New York for a year, including rent paid and a small allowance, scholarships to Villa Massimo in Italy, or to the International Art Centre in Paris. (Information about these schemes also through the Senate).

Indirect support includes the subsidising of centres such as Künstlerhaus Bethanien and the yet to be opened (autumn 1986) sculpture workshop in Wedding, financing the periodical 'Kunstblatt', buying works to be later exhibited by the Berlinische Galerie or the Berliner Kunstverein (in 1984 such buying totalled 200,000 DM), supporting group projects, (11 groups were subsidised in 1984 received together 120,000 DM7 and helping artists generally (in 1984 70,000 DM was set aside for this).

FURTHER FINANCIAL AID (Private)

The Karl Hofer Gesellschaft: 41, Telephone 8527081.
This organisation gives help to ex-Hochschule der Künste artists, has 16 studios available for artists which are rent free — payment required only for heating and electricity — awards scholarships, holds exhibitions, helps selbsthilfgalerien.

Karl Schmidt-Rotluff-Förderungsstiftung: Scholarships awarded to young artists, that is, younger then 35. Five artists chosen at one time.

Hans Hermann Stober: An individual art supporter in Berlin, who among other investments in the arts, encourages the exhibition of young artists' work in his gallery at Tempelhofer Ufer (Kutscherhaus)

Tetra Pak: This is a packing company which holds an art competition for Constructive/Concrete art. The first prize is worth 25,000 DM.

OTHER ADDRESSES WHICH MAY BE OF HELP

Hochschule der Künste: Ernst-Reuter Platz, 1000 Berlin 10, Telephone 3416051

Berufsuerband Bildener Küntler Giesebrechtstraße 11, 1000 Berlin 12, Telephone 8826115

ART and ARTISTS' ASSOCIATIONS

Arbeitsgemeinschaft Berliner Kunstamtleiter e.V., Oranienburger Straße 170, 1000 Berlin 26, Telephone 4022102/71. Association of Kunstamt directors.

Berufsverband Bildener Künstler Berlins: Giesebrechstraße 11, 1000 Berlin 12, Telephone 8826115. Berlin artists' union.

Berliner Künstler Bund: e.V. Wassertorstraße 11, 1000 Berlin 61, Telephone 61452421. Berlin office of the: **Deutsche Künstlerbund** e.V., Kurfürstendamm 65, 1000 Berlin 15, Telephone 8837323. West German artists' union.

Deutsche Verein Für Kunszwissenschaft e.V. Jebensstraße 1, 1000 Berlin 12, Telephone 3139932

Deutsche Werkbund e.v. Landersverband, Berlin, Hardenbergstraße 9, 1000 Berlin 12, Telephone 3138575

Förderkreisdes Antikenmuseums: Friends' organisation of the Antikenmuseum, contact c/o museum.

Freie Berliner Kunstausstellung e.V., Office for the organising of the annual exhibition of Berlin artists, Dernburgerstraße 19, 1000 Berlin 19, Telephone 4335111/43411821

Freunde des Museums Fur Deutsche Volkskunde: Friends' organisation of the Deutsche Volkskunde Museum, providing financial support, publishing information and facilitating student travel. Contact c/o the Museum.

Gesellschaft Zur Aktivierung von Kunst und Wissenschaft e.V. Schildhornstraße 74, 1000 Berlin 41, Telephone 7922244/7926044

Internationales Design Zentrum Berlin e.V. Wieland Staße 31, 1000 Berlin 12.

Interessengemeinschaft Berliner Kunsthändeler e.v. Ludwigkirchstraße 11a 1000 Berlin 15, Telephone 883.2643. Art dealers' association and publisher and editor of the periodical 'Kunstblatt'. A most, perhaps the most, important art association in Berlin.

Kaiser-Friedrich-Museums-Verein: Support for the painting and sculpture galleries at Dahlem; contact c/o Dahlem Museums.

Kunst-Dienst Der Evangelishen Kirche: Jebensstraße 3, 1000 Berlin 12, Telephone 3128096

Elvira Bach's studio in Kreuzberg

Kunstgeschichtliche Gesellschaft Zu Berlin: Arnimallee 23, 1000 Berlin 33, Telephone 8301218. Art History Society.

Neue Gesellschaft für Bildende Kunst e.v. Hardenbergstraße 9, 1000 Berlin 12, Telephone 316182.

Notgemeinschaft Der Deutschen Kunst e.v. Kurfürstendamm 66, 1000 Berlin 15, Telephone 3135839. Auctioneers' association.

Verband der Berliner Auktionatoren e.v. Kurfürstendamm 58, 1000 Berlin 15, Telephone 8836179. Auctioneer's association.

Verband Der Berliner Kunst Und Antiquitätenhändler e.v. Kurfürstendamm 58, 1000 Berlin 15, Telephone 3232046. Antique dealers' association.

Verein Berliner Künstler: Schöneberger Ufer 57, 1000 Berlin 30, Telephone 2612399. Berlin artists' association.

Verein Der Berliner Künstlerinnen e.v.: Warnemünder Straße 10a, 1000 Berlin 33, Telephone 8232760. Association of women artists.

Verein Berlinische Galerie: Friends' organisation of the Berlinische Galerie; an important association in Berlin. c/o Berlinische Galerie.

Vereine Der Freunde Und Föderer Des Berlin-Museums: Gierkplatz 9, 1000 Berlin 10, Friends association of the Berlin Museum. Contact c/o the museum.

Verein Für Kunsthandwerk Berlin e.V.: Pariser Straße 39, 1000 Berlin 15, Telephone 8813862. Berlin crafts' association.

Verein Der Freunde Der Nationalgalerie: A very important organisation in Berlin for the 'art scene'; the 'friends' support financially and make decisions about buying. Contact c/o Nationalgalerie.

Der Verein Der Freunde Der Preußischer Schlösser Und Garten: Friends' organisation supporting the palaces and gardens. Contact Charlottenburg Palace.

Verein Der Föderung Des Agyptischen Museums: Friends' organisation of the Egyptian Museum, c/o the Museum.

ARTISTS' MATERIALS

Ebeling: Fuggerstraße 43-45, 1000 Berlin 30, Telephone 211.4621
This is a No. 1 shop for artists' supplies in Berlin and carries an enormous variety of stock. Also carries specialist drawing and painting materials, a good selection of pencils, a huge variety of paper and materials for sculptors.

Arthur Lederer: Savignyplatz 9-10, 1000 Berlin 12, Telephone 312.4436.
Manufacturers of stage decorations, stocking textiles normally used for theatre and in 10-15 metre width, for example, fine muslin, muslin veiling, shirting, linen, tulle, foils, velours, glass tissue. Canvas as well.

Bernard Moock: Bleibtreustraße 4, 1000 Berlin 12, Telephone 3123060/3122190/3122745.
House-paint materials etc., school supplies, dried paints, terpentine, oils, Minimum quanitity 1-2 kg or 1 litre

Hermann Noack: Fehlerstraße 8, 1000 Berlin 41, Telephone 8216387/8211013.
World famous for sculptors. (Used for instance by Henry Moore).

Old Mole: Nostitzstraße 16-18, Kreuzberg.
Artists' supplies. Good for stretchers and oil paints. Cheaper.

Öta Farbenweld: Mindener Straße 2, 1000 Berlin 12, Telephone 3448052.
House-paints and brushes. Larger quantites. Cheaper.

Performance: Crellestraße 22, 1000 Berlin 62, Telephone 7818775.
Materials for the theatre. They also sell textiles in large amounts as off-cuts and thereby very cheaply.

Arnold Schaberow: Hardenbergstraße 19, 1000 Berlin 12, Telephone 312.4001.
Good general stock of artist supplies.

Schwarzmarkt: Geigergstraße 12, Schöneberg.
Good selection and cheaper. Also materials for sculpture.

Spitta & Leutz: Hohenzollerndamm 174, 1000 Berlin 31, Telephone 870531.

Branch at Knesebeckstraße 99, 1000 Berlin 12.
The other No. 1 shop for all artists' supplies, including painting, drawing, graphics materials; photography and reproduction materials; architectural and office supplies; equipment for screen printing; materials for sculpture.

Additional Suppliers

Paints/Farben
Gonis-Werke Kohlfurter Straße 41-43, 1000 Berlin 36, Telephone 6146052. Only school products; Tempera.

Gallery Furniture/Galeriebedarf

heller engel Bregenzer Straße 9, 1000 Berlin 15, Telephone 882 2882. Splints, mounting, frames, hanging, consultation.

Bild Rahmen K. Boche Kurfürstendamm 132, 1000 Berlin 31, Telephone 891.6492.

Galerie L. Sperlich: Blissestraße 54, 1000 Berlin 31, Telephone 8226180. Advice.

Transport/Kunsttransporte

Bergemann and Company, Invalidenstraße 50-51, 1000 Berlin 21, Telephone 394.5011. Telex: 302113

Knaver, Gustav, Pfalzburger Straße 19, 1000 Berlin 31, Telephone 860101. Telex: 0184414. and Gattlieb-Dunkel-Straße 20/21, 1000 Berlin 42, Telephone 7035030, Telex: 0184414. Also antique transport specialists.

Canvas/Leinwand

heller engel: Bregenzer Straße 9, 1000 Berlin 15, Telephone 882.2882

Pedestals/Objektsockel:

Bergmann and Company, Invalidenstraße 50-51, 1000 Berlin 21, Telephone 394.5011. Telex 302114.

Reynolds, M.P. Morgensternerstraße 1, 1000 Berlin 45, Telephone 772.2087.

Mounting/Passepartouts

Bergmann and Company: Invalidenstraße 50-51, 1000 Berlin 21. Telephone 394.5011, Telex 302113

heller engel: Bregenzer Straße 9, 1000 Berlin 15, Telephone 882.2882.

Wehner F. GmBH & Co. KG: Skalitzer Straße 68, 1000 Berlin 36, Telephone 612.5031.

Frames/Rahmen

Bergmann and Company, Invalidenstraße 50-51. 1000 Berlin 21, Telephone 394.5011, Telex 302113

heller engel: Bregenzer Straße 9, 1000 Berlin 15, Telephone 882.2882.

Flohr & Cie: Ritterstrße 11, 1000 Berlin 61.

Hever Haus, Lausitzer Straße 10,1000 Berlin 36

Keilrahmen Mühlenhaupt: Plannfer 95 II, 1000 Berlin 36, Telephone 691.2943.

Rahmenfabrik Berlin KG: Lankwitzer Straße 37, 1000 Berlin 42, Telephone 705.1077.

Rosemann and Jacobowski: Wasserterstraße 62, 1000 Berlin 61.

Scharte, Theodor GmBH, Reichenberger Straße 88, 1000 Berlin 36, Telephone 612.7091.

Wehner F. GmBH & Co. KG. Skalitzer Straße 68, 1000 Berlin 36, Telephone 612.5031.

Also framing by Menzel; Wolff; Wenau;Wormuth; Silberhaus Rahmen.

Insurance/Versicherung

Adler Feuerversicherung AG Leibnizstraße 3-4, 1000 Berlin 12, Telephone 34081.

heller engel: Bregenzer Straße 9, 1000 Berlin 15, Telephone 882.2882.

Voss, Richard Kurfürstendamm 64-65. 1000 Berlin 15, Telephone 881.6072/74

Display-cases/Vitrinen

Dogs & Schiller Schlesische Straße 20, 1000 Berlin 36, Telephone 612.2650.

heller engel Bregenzer Straße 9, 1000 Berlin 15, Telephone 882.2882.

Herrendorf & Kwee Kurfürstendamm 185, 1000 Berlin 15, Telephone 881.1817.

Kai Sien Kwee Kurfürstendamm 185, 1000 Berlin 15, Telephone 881.1817. Telex 183698.

For hardware: nails, wood, paints etc.
BAUHAUS

Several branches:
Gorkistraße 19, 1000 Berlin 27, Telephone 433.4074
Bayreuther Straße 3, 1000 Berlin 30, Telephone 211.7001
Kurfürstendamm 146, 1000 Berlin 31, Telephone 892.9039
Borussia Straße 22, 1000 Berlin 42, Telephone 752.5086
Tempelhofer-Weg 91, 1000 Berlin 47, Telephone 606.5014.

PHOTOGRAPHIC MATERIALS

For all materials: (retail)

Foto Meyer
Geisebergstraße 14, 1000 Berlin 30, Telephone 247087. Generally seen as the NO.1 photographic supplies shop.

Foto Wüstefeld

Grolmanstrße 36 (corner Kurfürstendamm). Also Kanstraße 117 and Schloßstraße 96. Telephone 883.7593/791.8888/881.9696

Wholesale

Bremaphot

Warehouse for professionals or retailers. Sells everything except cameras; cheaper rates for larger quantities. Selection better at retailers.

Fur further information
Redbox A handbook about photography and film in West Germany which contains a directory of useful addresses.

Photographers for art books, catalogues, exhibitions etc.

Günter Lepkowski, Friedrichstraße 217, 1000 Berlin 61, Telephone 251.3119.

Jochen Littkemann, Berlin's most well-known and respected art photographer concentrating on books and catalogues. Fasanenstraße 61, 1000 Berlin 15, Telephone 883.5473.

Hans Pieler, Jebensstraße 1, 1000 Berlin 12, Telephone 312.9019

Manfred M. Sackmann, specialising in exhibition openings. Telephone 691.1489.

Also the following: J. Anders, F. Friedrich, H.E. Kiessling, I. Lommatzsch, O. Reuter, P. Sticha, A. Weidling, H. Zenke.

Irene Fehling's studio

Fine Art Critics

Jürgen Beckelmann
Pfalzburger Straße 80,
1000 Berlin 15

Peter Hans Göpfert
Helgoländer Ufer 6,
1000 Berlin 21.

Rainer Höynck
Travnsteiner Straße 1,
1000 Berlin 30.

Hans Crhistoph Knebusch
2DF-Studio Berlin
Oberlandstraße 85-90.
1000 Berlin 42

Werner Langer
Ottot-Suhr-Allee 27,
1000 Berlin 10.

Enka Lippki
Xantener Straße 22,
1000 Berlin 15

Dorothea Neumeister
ReichsstraBe 105,
1000 Berlin 19.

Michael Mungesser
Hohenzollerndamm 14,
1000 Berlin 15.

Heinz Ohff
Grossbeerenstraße 57(A)
1000 Berlin 61.

Werner Rhode
Beerenstraße 66,
1000 Berlin 37.

Philip Peter Scmidt
Reichsstraße 82,
1000 Berlin 19.

Barbara Schnierle-Wien
bei T Scmidt
Bleibtreustraße 3
1000 Berlin 12.

Bernard Schulz
Brandenburgische Straße 6,
1000 Berlin 31.

Jeannot Simmon
Postfach 628,
1000 Berlin 15.

Angelika Stepken
Kurfürstenstraße 173,
1000 Berlin 30.

Verena Tafel
Friedrich-Franz-Straße 3,
1000 Berlin 42.

Roland H.Wiegenstein
Knesebeckstraße 20,
1000 Berlin 12.

Thomas Wulffen
Herrfurthstraße 7,
1000 Berlin 44.

Berlin Magazines for the fine arts and Berlin cultural programmes.

'Akademie Anzeiger'
Hanseatenweg 10, 1000 Berlin 21

'Berliner Kunstblatt'
Ludwigkirchstraße 11a, 1000 Berlin 15.
Lists monthly Berlin art exhibitions.

'Berliner Kultur Kalender'
Xanter Straße 5, 1000 Berlin 15

'Berlin Programm'
Postfach 330520
1000 Berlin 33

'Daidalos'
Schlüterstraße 42, 1000 Berlin 15

'Der Berliner Kulturführer'
Postfach 4007
1000 Berlin 30

'Kult-uhr'
Mittenwalder Straße 6,
1000 Berlin 61

'Kultur'
Europa-Center,
1000 Berlin 30

'Kultur Politik'
Köthener Straße 44,
1000 Berlin 61

'Kunst und Museen in Berlin'
Oranienburger Straße 170,
1000 Berlin 26

'Kunst ist in Berlin'
Köthener Straße 44,
1000 Berlin 61.

'Tip'
Postdamer Straße 96,
1000 Berlin 30

'Zitty'
Schluterstraße 39,
1000 Berlin 12

THE STRUCTURE OF ARTS ADMINISTRATION
Der Senator Für Kulturelle Angelegenheiten

The main body financing and administering the arts in West Berlin is the Senator für Kulturelle Angelegenheiten which finances and administers all state-funded artistic ventures. The aim of the Senate's work is to thereby make possible and encourage the arts in West Berlin but in no way to influence or censor. All artistic activity financed by the Senate remains as artistically autonomous as if it were not financially supported.

The address of the Senate is the Europa Center, 1000 Berlin 30, Telephone 21233200. It is divided into sections of the fine arts; music; theatre; literature; festivals; 'free groups' (for example, 'off' music and theatre, experimental groups); media; film; 'Kultur Export', which is the organising of exhibitions or presentations of Berlin art elsewhere or exchanges etc., museums; palaces and gardens; the Preußischer Kulturbesitz; churches and associations.

KUNSTÄMTE

The Senate finances and administers the arts in West Berlin as a whole, but as Berlin is divided into districts — somewhat akin to the English boroughs — each area also has its own Kunstamt, an art board or council, which organises exhibitions, readings, concerts and so on in the area. Contact addresses and telephone numbers are listed below:

Charlottenburg: Otto-Suhr-Allee 100, 1000 Berlin 10, Telephone 3430-1

Kreuzberg: Yorckstraße 4, 1000 Berlin 61, Telephone 25883300

Neukölln: Karl-Marx-Straße 83, 1000 Berlin 44, Telephone 68091.

Reinickendorf: Eichborndamm 215/239, 1000 Berlin 26, Telephone 41921

Schöneberg: John-F-Kennedy-Platz, 1000 Berlin 62, Telephone 7832301.

Spandau: Carl-Schurz-Straße 2-6, 1000 Berlin 20, Telephone 3303-1

Steglitz: Schloßstraße 80, 1000 Berlin 41, Telephone 7904-1

Tempelhof: Tempelhofer Damm 165, 1000 Berlin 42, Telephone 7560300

Tiergarten: Turmstraße 35, 1000 Berlin 21, Telephone 39051

Wedding: Müllerstraße 146/147, 1000 Berlin 31, Telephone 8689-1

Zehlendorf: Kirchstraße 1/3, 1000 Berlin 37, Telephone 807-1

BERLINER KULTURAT: The Berliner Kulturat includes about 30 cultural associations, each member organisation paying in. Initiatives, projects and individual members may also join. The purpose of the Kulturat is to help and make known cultural activities in West Berlin at base level, a mirror at the other end of what the Senate does at the official or established level. The Kulturat works closely with the Kunstämte, to help their projects be known and receive support. The address of the Kulturat is Köthener Straße 44, 1000 Berlin 61, and telephone number 261.1192. Members are listed below:

Arbeitsgemeinschaft Berliner Kunstamtsleiter e.V (Arge)

Berliner Arbeitskreis Film e.V. (BAF).

Berufsverband Bildender Künstler Berlins e.V. (BBK) in der Gewerkschaft Kunst im DGB, LBZ Berlin

Bund Deutscher Architekten — BDA Berlin e.V.
Bund Deutscher Grafik-Designer, Gruppe Berlin e.V. (BDG)
Bund Deutscher Kunsterzieher e.V. (BDK)
Bundesfachgruppe Bühne Film Fernsehen in der DAG, LV Berlin (BFF/DAG).
Club der Filmjournalisten Berlin e.V.
Deutsche Journalisten Union in der IG Druck und Papier, LBZ Berlin (dju)
Deutscher Komponisten Verband, Sektion Berlin (DKV)
Deutscher Künstlerbund e.V. (DKB)
Deutscher Musikerverband in der Gewerkschaft Kunst im DGB, LBZ, Berlin (LMV)
Deutsche Orchestervereinigung e.V. in der Gewerkschaft Kunst im DGB, LBZ Berlin (DOV)
Deutscher Werkbund Berlin e.V. (DWB)
Dramaturgische Gesellschaft (dg)
Freunde der deutschen Kinemathek e.V.
GEDOK-Berlin (Gemeinschaft der Künsterinnen und Kunstfreunde e.V.
Gewerkschaft der Musikerzieher und konzertierender Künstler in der Gewerkschaft Kunst im DGB, LBZ Berlin (GDMK)
Journalisten-Verband Berlin im Deutschen Journlisten-Verband (JVB)
Neue Gesellschaft für Bildende Kunst e.V. (NGBK)
Neue Gesellschaft für Literatur (NGL) e.V. (NGL)
Rundfunk-Fernseh-Film-Union im DGB, Verband Film (RFFU/Film)
Rundfunk-Fernseh-Film-Union im DGB, Verband RIAS (RFFU/RIAS)
Rundfunk-Fernseh-Film Union im DGB, Verband SFPB (RFFU/SFB)
Verband der deutschen Kritiker e.V.
Verband Deutscher Musikerzieher und konzertierender Künstler, Landesverband Berlin e.V. (VDMK)
Verband deutscher Musikschulen e.V., Landsgruppe Berlin (VDM)
Verband deutscher Schriftsteller in der IG Druck und Papier, LBZ Berlin (VS)
Verband Deutscher Schulmusikerzieher, Landesverband Berlin e.V. (VDS)
Verein der ausländischen Presse in Berlin (1951) e.V.

Arts' Prizes

For a complete list of prizes awarded in all the arts in Berlin, or West Germany, refer to the *Deutsche Handbuch der Kultur Preis*. To find out which libraries hold this handbook telephone the Berliner Gesamt Katalog. 266.2880.

ARTS TUITION

For the best arts tition in the fine arts, music, theatre, architecture, design, and teaching the arts:
Hochschule der Künste, Hardenbergstraße 33, 1000 Berlin 12 Telephone 31852204.
For foreign students: Postal address: Auslandsamt. Postfach 126720, 1000 Berlin 12.
Freie Universität Berlin: Altensteiner 40, 1000 Berlin 33, Telephone 8381.
Press and information office: Telephone 8382746.

Lette Schule-Berufsfachschule für Fotografie, Grafik und Mode, Viktoria Luise Platz 6, Telephone 21994131.
School for photography, graphic art and fashion design.
Staatliche Fachschule für Optik und Fofotechnik: Einsteinufer 43-53, 1000 Berlin 10, Telephone 31832681/0.
Concentrates on the technical aspects of photograpy.
Technische Fachhochschule Berlin: Luxemburger Straße 10, 1000 Berlin 65, Telephone 45041
Technische Universität Berlin: Straße des 17 Juni 135, 1000 Berlin 12 Telephone 3141 or information/press 3142919/3143922
Werkstatt für Photographie der Volkshochschule Kreuzberg: Friedrichstraße 210, 1000 Berlin 61, Telephone 25887866. See photography galleries.
The Volkshochschulen provide first rate continuing education tuition for amateurs.
Each district has such tuition offering a variety of courses in most of the arts: Addresses below:
Die Volkshochschulen
Tiergarten, 21, Turmstra 72. Telephone 3905 338
Wedding, 65, Ravenestr 12. Telephone 457 3051/3050
Kreuzberg, 61 Friedrichstr 210, Telephone 2588 7868/5861
Charlottenburg, 19, Heerstr 12, Telephone 3005 371/372
Spandau, 20, Hohenzollernring, 15, Telephone 3303/2532
Neukölln, 44, Rollbergstrm 7, Telephone 68 09 2433/3304.
Tempelhof, 42, Burgemeisterstr 34, Telephone 7560/408/326
Schöneberg, 30, Barbarossaplatz 5, Telephone 783/2323
Wilmersdorf, 31, Fehrbelliner Platz 4, Telephone 8689/371
Zehlendorf: 37, Markgrafenstr, 3, Telephone 807/2685.
Steglitz, 41, Schloßstr, 36/37. Telephone 79 94 2373/2372
Reinickendorf, 27, Buddestr, 21, Telephone 4192 6227/6226
Heimvolkshochschule, Schloß Glienicke Königstraße 1000 Berlin 39
An advice centre about courses is at Bredtschneiderstraße 5, 1000 Berlin 19, Telephone 3016047.

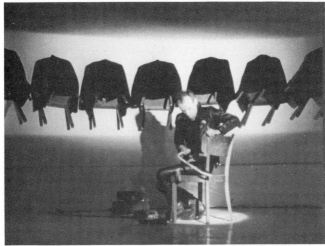

Jurgen Klauke in performance at Kunstlerhaus Bethanien

MUSIC

Music in Berlin is important and Berlin is one of the world's centres — some would say the centre — for European music. It boasts not only the Berlin Philharmonic with its chief conductor Herbert von Karajan but offers an array of top international conductors and soloists throughout the season. If that is not enough there are two other orchestras, the Radio Symphonie Orchester and the Symphonisches Orchester Berlin and a feast of chamber ensembles and choirs. A week's musical programme in Berlin will offer audiences anything from Baroque Chamber music performed on original instruments to contemporary experimental groups. Berlin has quality and quantity in its musical variety.

THE ORCHESTRAS

Berliner Philharmonisches Orchester
The Berlin Philharmonic

Matthäikirchstrase 1, 1000 Berlin 30.
Telephone 25488-0
Chief conductor and Artistic Director: Herbert von Karajan.
Director: Dr Wolfgang Stresemann
The orchestra now celebrates 103 years of musical supremacy. Herbert von Karajan is the fourth chief conductor following Hans von Bülow, Arthur Nikisch and Wilhelm Furtwängler. During the post war years Serjiu Celibidache was important in the 'rebuilding' of the orchestra.

The orchestra has enjoyed a tradition of famous composers conducting their works, including Johannes Brahms, Richard Strauss, Peter Tchaikowsky, Edvard Grieg, Gustav Mahler, Igor Stravinsky, Maurice Ravel and Paul Hindemith.

At present the orchestra has 121 members. It gives around 82 concerts in West Berlin each year and about 30 on tour. Since 1963 the home of the Berlin Philharmonic has been the Philharmonie, designed by Professor Hans Scharoun. The orchestra is surrounded by seating for 2400 people set in a circular form, Scharoun being inspired by noticing that wherever music is played people spontaneously form a circule around the musicians to listen. It is a beautiful auditorium and the acoustics are said to be among the best, of not the best, in the world.

Guest conductors who regularly appear with the orchestra include Claudio Abbado, Daniel Barenboim, Zubin Mehta, Seiji Ozawa and James Levine. And there are life-time friends such as Yehudi Menuhin who first performed with the orchestra at 12 years of age, or the late Karl Böhm, a friend until his death in 1981 and famous for his recordings with the orchestra of Mozart's symphonies.

Such is the feeling of Berliners for their main orchestra that news about it will always make media headlines in West Berlin.

Radio-Symphonie-Orchester-Berlin
Berlin Radio Symphony Orchestra

Kaiserdamm 26, 1000 Berlin 19,
Telephone 302.7243
Chief conductor: Riccardo Chailly
Director: Dr Peter Ruzicka.
This 100 member orchestra gives around 32 Symphony concerts in Berlin each year, performing half in the Philharmonie and half in the large recording studio of the S.F.B. The R.S.O is the official broadcasting orchestra in Berlin. It accompanies choirs and, like the Berlin Philharmonic, makes recordings and goes on tour. Different musicians from the R.S.O. make up Chamber Ensembles which are held in the Otto-Braun-Saal of the Staatsbibliothek. The ensembles are organised by the director and chamber concerts occur about seven times each year. The R.S.O. has the task of cultivating lesser known works from past and present.

Symphonisches Orchester Berlin e.V.
Berlin Symphony Orchestra

Kurfürstendamm 237, 1000 Berlin 15,
Telephone 8834094
Chief Condutor: Daniel Nazareth
Director: Norbert Thomas.
The 65 member Symphonisches Orchester Berlin was founded in 1966. It performs about 28 concerts each year, serves as the orchestra for Hochschule der Künste student conductors and accompanies larger Berlin choirs. Programmes are usually of the more familiar classical or romantic music.

Chamber Ensembles
Some of the major ensembles are listed below:

Baroque Orchester

Arnold-Knoblauch-Ring 64,
1000 Berlin 39,
Telephone 805.1418
Conductor: Konrad Latte

Brandis Quartet

Eichenallee 5a
1000 Berlin 19,
Telephone 302.3600

Die 12 Cellisten des Berliner Philharmonischen Orchesters

Contact: Rudolf Weinsheimer
Berliner Straße 27,
1000 Berlin 37,
Telephone 811.7027
12 cellists from the Berlin Philharmonic.

Gruppe Neue Musik Berlin

Contact: Gerald Humel
Claudius Straße 12,
1000 Berlin 21,
Telephone 391.1929.
Mainly play twentieth century music and also perform music composed by members of the group.

Haydn Kammerorchester

Contact: Helmut Link
Göllweg 17,
1000 Berlin 42,
Telephone 741.1268.

Kreuzberger Streichquartet

Contact: Hans Joachim Creiner
Tegeler Weg 105,
1000 Berlin 10,
Telephone 344.3705.
This group was formed by music students still studying at the Hochschule der Künste. Their debut about a year later was such a success that they continued performing and are now one of the top European chamber ensembles.

Musikalische Compagney

Contact: Holger Eichhorn
Dresdener Straße 12,
1000 Berlin 36,
Telephone 614.6225.
Perform pre-Bach European music on original instruments.

The Tiergarten near the Reichstag — symposium of Berlin Sculpture

Philharmonisches Duo

Contact: Klaus Stolll
Xantener Straße 15,
1000 Berlin 15,
Telephone 881.1705.
Musicians from the Berlin Philharmonic.

Philharmonisches Octet Berlin

Contact: Professor Paul Rainer Zepperitz
Max Eythstraße 35,
1000 Berlin 33,
Telephone 832.5030
Musicians from the Berlin Philharmonic. Famous throughout its
50 years existence; composers such as Blacher, Hindemith,
Stockhausen and Isang Yun have composed especially for the
Octet.

Freunde Guter Musik Berlin e.V

Erkelenzdamm 11-13 B IV, 1000 Berlin 36, Telephone 652702.
This is an important musical association in Berlin, formed two
years ago to further interest in new and experimental music, not
only experiemental classical but also rock, jazz and avant garde
and particularly the areas between them, for instance the area
between 'E musik' ('Ernst Musik' or serious music) and 'U musik'
('Unterhaltung Musik' or background music). The juxtaposition of
music with other art forms, the fine arts or performance for example, is also a particular interest.
Music on Sunday Afternoons:
In addition to organising festivals and concerts the Freunde also
offer a series of workshop concerts held monthy, or thereabouts,
at 5pm at the Institut Unzeit - address above. The Institut is a
Kreuzberg artists' loft. These Sunday afternoon concerts are
varied. Mostly composers perform their own works and many international composers and musicians have participated.

Choirs

Berliner Sängerbund is the umbrella organisation for about 80
amateur choirs and has 5000 or so members. The address is:
Kurfürstendamm 237, 1000 Berlin 15, Telephone 883.1697.
The main Berlin choirs are:
Berliner Konzert-Chor e.V.
Lietzenburger Straße 51,
Telephone 245.001
Conductor Fritz Weisse
Founded in 1954 this choir gives about four concerts per season
and also performs in hospitals, prisons, parks, as well as touring.
Varied programme — from Bach to Pfitzner.

Chor der St. Hedwigs-Kathedrale

Kolonnenstraße 38,
1000 Berlin 62,

Telephone 784.3061.
Conductor: Roland Bader
Choir of the Catholic Church. Repertoire from classical to contemporary. Four/five Philharmonie concerts each year, as well as other concerts and church music.

Philharmonischer Chor Berlin e.V.

Flensburger Straße 21,
Telephone 391.3693.
Conductor: Professr Uwo Gronostay.
Founded 1882. Four/five concerts per season. Works together with the Berlin Philharmonic.

RIAS-Kammerchor

RIAS Berlin Musikabteilung (RIAS Berlin Music Department)
Kufsteiner Straße 69,
1000 Berlin 62
Telephone 85031
Leader: Professor Uwe Gronostay.
Concerts,touring, media performances. This is the only professional choir apart from the Deutsche Oper Choir.

Sing-Akademie zu Berlin

Lynarstraße 1A
1000 Berlin 33,
Telephone 892.6001
Director: Professor Hans Hilsdorf
Four to six concerts per season in Berlin. The choir also tours. It performs mostly religious works of J.S. Bach and pre-twentieth century works.

Useful addresses

Akademie der Künste
Hanseatenweg,
1000 Berlin 21,
Telephone: 391.1031
Contacts and concerts.

Deutscher Akademischer Austauschdienst (DAAD)
Steinplatz 2,
1000 Berlin 12,
Telephone: 310.461
Scholarships to non-Germans for a year in Berlin.

Deutscher Komposisten Verband
Bergengruen Straße 28,
1000 Berlin 38,
Telephone: 801.8065
Composer's Association.

Deutsches Musik Archiv
Gärtner Straße 25-32,

1000 Berlin 45,
Telephone: 771.6026
Holds the collection of *all* recordings made in Germany.

Elektronisches Studio
c/o Technisches Universität,
For electronic productions and concerts.

Gesellschaft der Freunde des Berliner Philharmonischen Orchester
Matthäikirchstraße 1,
1000 Berlin 30.
Friends of the Berlin Philharmonic. Fund raising, functions, for further information contact the general director of the orchestra, Dr Streseman. The Deutsche Oper has a similar friends organisation; contact address/information c/o the Deutsche Oper.

GEMA Gesellschaft für musikalische Aufführungs und mechanische Vervielfältigungs rechte
Copyright and all legal matters.
Two addresses: The main one is Bayreuther StraBe 37/38,
1000 Berlin 30,
Telephone 21041
Serving the Berlin districts: Ernst-Reuter-Platz 10,
1000 Berlin 10
Telephone 341.061.

Hochschule der Künste

Ernst-Reuter-Platz 10, 1000 Berlin 10, Telephone 3185-0
For all tuition of a professional standard. For amateur tuition, see district music schools.

Künstlerhaus Bethanien

Mariannenplatz 2, 1000 Berlin 36, Telephone 614.8010
Concerts. Rooms for DAAD scholarship holders.

Landesmusikrat Berlin

Kaiserdamm 23, 1000 Berlin 19, Telephone 301.8510.
Lobbying association for music in Berlin, for example financial support, music in schools etc.

Der Seantor für Kulturelle Angelegenheiten

Europa-Center, 1000 Berlin 30, Telephone 2123.3200
For all state financed and administered musicmatters.

Staatliches Institut für Musikforschung

Tiergarten Straße 1, 1000 Berlin 30, Telephone 254.810
Director: Professor Reinecke
State Institue for Music Research

VDMK Verband Deutsche Musikerzieher Konzerterender Künstler

Bismarckstraße 73, 1000 Berlin 19, Telephone 312.3677
Association for musicians and teachers of music. Organisers
also of the *Studio Neue Musik Berlin* for the encouragement of
new muic' (that is to say from about Schönberg on). Concerts are
held regularly.

Vereinigung der Freunde und Förderer der Musikinstrumenten-sammlung Berlin e.V.

Bundesallee 1-12, 1000 Berlin 15, Telephone 881.7835.
Collectors of musical instruments association.

For information about concerts:
The 'Konzertführer' (correctly known as the 'Fuhrer durch die
Konzertsäle Berlins) publishes the full programme of classical
concerts.
Publishing Office: Bundesallee 1-12, 1000 Berlin 15, Telephone
883.8128
See also 'Tip' and 'Zitty' and the newspapers.

Concert Agents.

Hans Adler

August-Viktoria-Straße 64, 1000 Berlin 33,
Telephone 825 6255/825 6160.
For classical music.

Concertino

Luzerner Straße 14B, 1000 Berlin 45,
Telephone 817.3364.

Music Critics

Hans Heinz Stuckenschmidt

Winklerstraße 22, 1000 Berlin 33.
Writes for the Frankfurter Allgemeine 2eitung

Helmut Kotschenreuther and Sybil Mahlke — both critics for Der Tagespiegel.

Klaus Geitel Critic on Die Welt and Berliner Morgenpost.

Main places for classical concerts

Akademie der Künste
Hanseatenweg 10, 1000 Berlin 21, Telephone 391.1031

Hochschule der Künste
Larger concert hall; corner Fasanenstraße and
Hardenbergstraße.
Smaller concert hall: Fasanenstraße 1.

Both Berlin 12.
Telephone 318.52374

Philharmonie
Matthäikirchstraße 1, 1000 Berlin 30, Telephone 254.880.

Staatsbibliothek, Otto-Braun-Saal.
Potsdamer Straße 33, 1000 Berlin 30, Telephone 266.2586.

Deutschlandhalle
Messedamm 26, 1000 Berlin 19, Telephone 3038-1

International Congress Centre
Internationles Congress Centrum — I.C.C.
Messedamm 26, 1000 Berlin 19, Telephone 3038-1

Large Broadcasting Hall at SFB
Masurenallee 8-14, 1000 Berlin 19, Telephone 3081.

Alte TU-Mensa
Hardenbergstraße 34, 1000 Berlin 12, Telephone 311.2233

Amerika Haus
Hardenbergstraße 21-24, 1000 Berlin 12, Telephone 819.7661

Audimax an der F.U.
Garystraße/Corner Boltzmannstraße, 1000 Berlin 33.

The British Centre
Hardenbergstraße 20, 1000 Berlin 12, Telephone 310176

Cafe Einstein
Kurfürstenstraße 58, 1000 Berlin 30, Telephone 261.5096.
For chamber and solo performances.

Centre Francais
Müllerstraße 74, 1000 Berlin 65, Telephone 418.1418/418.1766

Deutschlandhaus
Stresemannstraße 90, 1000 Berlin 61. Telephone 261.1046

Eissporthalle
Jaffestraße, 1000 Berlin 19. Telephone 3038-1

Ernst-Reuter-Saal
Eichborndamm 215-239, 1000 Berlin 52.

Fontane-Haus
Wilhelmsruher Damm 142c, 1000 Berlin 26

Forum Kreuzberg
Eisenbahnstraße 27, 1000 Berlin 36, Telephone 618.2222

Gemeinschaftshaus Gropiusstadt
Bat-Yam-Platz 1, 1000 Berlin 47, Telephone 680.92431

Künstlerhaus Bethanien
Mariannenplatz 2, 1000 Berlin 36, Telephone 614.8010/614.9021.

Rias Berlin, Studio 10,
Kurfsteiner Straße 69, 1000 Berlin 62, Telephone 8503-1

Theater des Westens
Kantstraße 12, 1000 Berlin 12, Telephone 312.1022

Urania
Kleistraße 13/14, 1000 Berlin 30, Telephone 24902/2491

Concerts are also often performed in churches. For information about church concerts telephone 319.00180/1.

Each district Kunstamt also organises concerts, held in various places. Telephone Kunstämte for information.

Shops and Libraries

The best libraries for books on music are:

The Amerika Gedenkbibliothek

Blücherplatz 1, 1000 Berlin 61, Telephone 69050

The Music Library at the Hochschule der Künste

Fasanenstraße 1, 1000 Berlin 12, Telephone 3185.2344

Staatsbibliothek

Potsdamer Straße 33, 1000 Berlin, Telephone 266-1

The two main music shops are:

Bote and Bock

Hardenburgstraße 9a, 1000 Berlin 12, Telephone 312.3081
Open Monday-Friday 9-6.30, Saturday 9-1.
Sheet music and books. Classical, rock, pop, folk, jazz. Music magazines.

Musik-riedel

Uhlandstraße 38, 1000 Berlin 15, Telephone 882.7395
Open Monday-Friday 8-6, Saturday 8-1.
Sheet music, records, books, instruments, antiquariat.

Also:

Gelbe Musik

Schaperstraße 11, 1000 Berlin 15, Telephone 211.3145/3962
Open Monday-Saturday 11-6.
Specialist record shop for experimental, avant garde music. Small

labels independently made and not mass produced are also available. At times also a gallery with exhibitions and/or concerts.

Canzone

Savignyplatz 5, 1000 Berlin 12, Telephone 312.4027
Open Monday-Friday 9.30-6.30, Saturday 9.30
Folk music and books.

Also see jazz section and list of bookshops in the literature section.

DISTRICT MUSIC SCHOOLS

Each of the 12 districts organises its own concerts and music festivals (this in addition to the already enormous variety to enjoy) and runs a music school — addresses below:

Charlottenburg Music School

Platanenallee 16, 1000 Berlin 19, Telephone 3005-1.

Kreuzberg Music School

Wasswetorstraße 4, 1000 Berlin 61, Telephone 2588-3107

Neukölln Music School

Weserstraße 13, 1000 Berlin, Telephone 68092626;

Reinickendorf Music School

Emmentaler Straße 69, 1000 Berlin 51, Telephone 41924336

Schöneberg Music School

Grunewaldstraße 6-7, 1000 Berlin 62, Telephone 738.3033.

Spandau Music School

Hohenzollerndamm 15, 1000 Berlin 20, Telephone 33032130.

Steglitz Music School

Graberstraße 4, 1000 Berlin 41, Telephone 79042381.

Tempelhof Music School

Wolfsburger Weg 13-19, 1000 Berlin 42, Telephone 4573052/3833.

Tiergarten Music School

Turmstraße 75, 1000 Berlin 21, Telephone 3905-1.

Wedding Music School

Ruheplatz 4, 1000 Berlin 65, Telephone 4573052/3833.

Wilmersdorf Music School

Fehrbelliner Platz 4, 1000 Berlin 31, Telephone 868.97781.

Zehlendorf Music School

Martin-Buber-Straße 21, 1000 Berlin 37, Telephone 807.2077.

Music Festivals

The main music festival is part of the Berliner Festwochen — the Berlin Festival Weeks — in September. The Jazz festival, also organised by the Berliner Festspiele is usually held in November. For both see section on Festivals.
There are also smaller music festivals:

Insel Musik a festival of international contemporary music for composers and musicians. Contact: Erhard Grosskopf, Telephone 216.5238.

Invention a festival of electronic music. Contact: Technische Universität, Straße des 17 Juni 135, 1000 Berlin 12, Telephone 3141.

Hurformen an annual or biannual festival held in Künstlerhaus Bethanien. The usual lines between the different arts are bridged; composers work with poets or artists for instance. Thematic expressions are explored. Contact: Eberhard Blum, Künstlerhaus Bethanien, Mariannenplatz 2, 1000 Berlin 36, Telephone 614.8010/01

Jazz in the Garden Jazz performed in the sculpture garden of the Nationalgalerie during June-July.

VDMK Bach Tage Mainly a Bach festival but not exclusively. Usually held in the first half of July (Pays to book early).

Foundations and competitions:

Akademie des Berliner Philharmonischen Orchesters e.V. Institut der Herbert von Karajan Stiftung.

The von Karajan Foundation was created by Herbert von Karajan and is financially supported by the state and private industry. The Akademie provides tuition for two years, or thereabouts, where young gifted musicians are taught by members of the Berlin Philharmonic and are given opportunities to play as members of the orchestra. About 30 people are chosen each year by auditioning before the full orchestra. The course is open to non-Germans.
   The Foundation also holds an **International Conductors' Competition**, held in Berlin every two years. It is entitled the Internationale Dirigenten Wetbewerbs der Herbert von Karajan Stiftung.
   For both the Akademie and the conductors' competition contact Professor Werner, Thäarichon am Waldhaus 34, 1000 Berlin 38, Telephone 803.6152.

Gotthard-Schierse-Stiftung

This foundation gives the opportunity for young chamber ensembles to perform and receive a write-up in the Berlin papers, a means of gaining both public and press experience. The contact address is Bundesallee 1-12, 1000 Berlin 15, Telephone 883.8128.

Steinway Competition for young pianists

For young pianists under 17 years. Held each year on November 18. Contact: Steinway Company, Hardenbergstraße 9, 1000 Berlin 12.

JAZZ IN BERLIN

With, perhaps, Köln, Berlin is the No 1 city for jazz in West Germany today. Its Jazz Festival, for instance, is internationally of great interest. Listed below is some of the more important jazz information.

Free Music Production is a musician's collective like the London Musician's Collective, which organises concerts and festivals, as well as making records. The two important festivals to watch out for organised by the FMP are:

Workshop Freie Musik which is held for 5 days around Easter time and concentrates on free jazz.

Total Music Meeting is the other festival which is held in November and runs parallel to the Berlin Jazz Festival. It is held in Quartier Latin.
Both festivals have German and international musicians participating. Generally there are a great variety of jazz concerts to

Performance in the backyard of the former 1/61 gallery

be heard in Berlin and concerts are usually full. 'Tip' and 'Zitty' are good guides to what's on. Groups change of course but two internationally renowned performers to look out for are pianist Alexander von Schlippenbach and percussionist Sven-Ake Johansson.

The jazz shop in Berlin is **Jazz Cock** which stocks all kinds of jazz from traditional to free, as well as records made by FMP. The shop is run by Dieter Hahne and the address is Behaimstraße 4, 1000 Berlin 10, Telephone 341.5447.

Main Places to hear Jazz:
Flöz Nassauesche Straße 37, 1000 Berlin 31, Telephone 861.1000

Passions Kirche Marheineke Platz (Kreuzberg) 1000 Berlin 61. International bands.

Quartier Latin, Potsdamer Straße 96, 1000 Berlin 30, Telephone 261.3707.

Quasimodo Corner Fasanenstraße and Kant Straße, 1000 Berlin 12 (next to Theater des Westens.)
Also international bands.
Sometimes jazz concerts at Cafe Einstein, Gasthaus Max and Moritz, the Hochschule der Künste, Metropole, the Philharmonie and the universities.

Jazz Front Berlin

Franckenstraße 2, 1000 Berlin 30, Telephone 216.1747
A non-profit association of musicians committed to improving the financial, performing, technical and management circumstances for jazz musicians in Berlin.

Rock, Pop, Blues, Folk....

London has always been seen as the No. 1 capital for rock music but today Berlin could be considered on a par and what is 'in' elsewhere in Europe is already 'out' in both London and Berlin. There are about 1000 rock groups in West Berlin, a relatively larger number than in any other European city which reflects West Berlin as very much a city for youth. Adding to that figure the jazz, blues, and folk groups the number would be increased to well over 1200.

West Berlin in West Germany's trend-setter, the home of the avant-garde. To characterise the trend in West Berlin would be to say that it is no trend, even anti-trend. West-Berlin's style is unceasing experimentation, fast change, a feeling for the new and simultaneity of art forms, for instance the combination of jazz and performance or dance and electronic music.

It is important for a group or individual performers to present an original quality; the number of groups, the tough competition and the critical Berlin public make this test of fame not to mention survival. Financial support from the Berlin Senate is concentrated upon improving the overall scene, for instance renovating venues, not in subsidising individual groups or performers.

Berlin Rock News: This is an annual prize worth 10,000 DM given by the Senate to a rock band or soloist living in Berlin. Runner-up prizes worth 2500 DM and 1000 DM respectively are also awarded. Those wishing to apply should send one cassette of three pieces with a photo and written information about the group/soloist. The cassette should not be a studio recording and groups under contract are excluded from applying, as is a group or soloist who have previously received a prize of 10,000 DM or more. The winners are decided by jury. For further information write to the Senator für Kulturelle Angelegenheiten IV E Europe Center, 1000 Berlin 30 or telephone 2123.3278.

Some major bands and soloists in 1984 and 1985 were:
Nena (Pop), Spliff (Rock), George Kranz (Rock), Ulla Meineke Band (Rock), Udo Lindenberg (Rock), and Tangerine Dream (Rock).

Useful organisations for rock, blues, folk etc with contact addresses and phone numbers.

AG-Song Triftstraße 54, 1000 Berlin 65, Telephone 461.6230 or Niebuhrstraße 62, 1000 Berlin 12, Telephone 323.9009
Organises get-togethers, workshops, concerts in a different city of the BRD each year.

Abeitsgrappe Moabit-Musik-Tage Wielefstraße 32, 1000 Berlin 21, Telephone 396.2613.
Music festivals.

Abeitskreis für Folkmusik Berlin Egidystraße 24, 1000 Berlin 21.
Folk musicians club.

Berliner Brettl, Niebuhrstraße 62, 1000 Berlin 12, Telephone 323.9009.
Alternative music.

Blues Co-operative Berlin, Am Hegewinkel 20, 1000 Berlin 37, Telephone 813.1665.
Blues festivals and workshops.

Burger-Initiative für Musik und Kunst, Niebuhrstraße 62, 1000 Berlin 12, Telephone 323.9009
Music and art initiatives.

Es-Musik-Initiative, Brusendorfer Straße 20, 1000 Berlin 44, Telephone 687.4486/642.3255
Rock for Amnesty International, anti-drugs festival, peace festivals etc.

German Blues Circle e.V. für Berlin, Reichenberger Straße 33a, 1000 Berlin 36, Telephone 618.4948.
Blues' Club.

Frauenmusikzentrum härm und hust Oranienstraße 189, Telephone 785.7915/783.2810.
Womens' music centre.

Rehearsal Space

Liberdastraße 14, 1000 Berlin 44, Telephone 623.4559
Studio and rehearsal rooms available for any length of time with/without equipment.

Tuition
Courses in the use of the synthesiser

Teltower Straße 29, 1000 Berlin 20, Telephone 331.3748/802.8461.

Rock music tuition for beginners to professionals at Widder Studio.

Albestraße 16, 1000 Berlin 41, Telephone 851.7950.

Agents and Managers

Kunstlerie Brutkasten e.V.
Peter Jakk, Fregestraße, 7a, 1000 Berlin 41, Telephone 851.7753.
Thomas Hundsatz, Donaustraße 6, 1000 Berlin 44, Telephone 623.8327.

Further information

See the annual handbook entitled **Rock City.**

Main addresses for live pop, rock, blues, folk...

Ballhaus Tiergarten, Perleberger Straße 62, 1000 Berlin 21, Telephone 394.3081.
Open from 6pm, programme from 8pm on. Anything and everything.

Go-In, Bleibtreustraße 17, 1000 Berlin 12, Telephone 881.7218.
Open 8pm, programme 9pm on. International folk, cabaret.

Irish Harp Pub, Giesebrechtstraße 15, 1000 Berlin 12, Telephone 882.7739
Programme from 9pm. Irish folk music.

Irish Pub im Europe-Center, Tauenzienstraße/Breitscheidplatz, 1000 Berlin 30, Telephone 262.1634.
Programme from 9pm. Folk, jazz, rock, soul.

Jazzkeller, Breitenbachplatz 8, 1000 Berlin 31, Telephone 824.4144
Open 8pm, programme 9pm on. Rock, rock 'n roll, blues, funk.

Joe's Bierhaus, Theodor-Heuss-Platz, 1000 Berlin 19, Telephone 301.7091/301.7092.
Open 11am, programme 9pm on. Traditional rock.

Joe am Ku'Damm, Kurfürstendamm 225/226, 1000 Berlin 15, Telephone 883.7873.
Programme from 9pm. Variety of pop music.

Kant Kino Kantstraße 54, 1000 Berlin 12, Telephone 312.5047.
Rock.

Loft Nollendorfplatz 5, 1000 Berlin 30, Telephone 216.2787.
Programme from 9pm. Rock, innovative music.

Metropole Musikpalast, Nollendorfplatz 5, 1000 Berlin 30,
Telephone 216.4122.
Open 6pm, programme 9pm on. Rock and pop. Discotheque.

Quasimodo, Kantstraße 12a, 1000 Berlin 12, Telephone 312.8086.
Open from 8pm, programme 10pm on. Jazz, blues, rock.

Villa Kreuzberg Freizeit-und Kommunikationszentrum,
Kreuzbergstraße 62, 1000 Berlin 61, Telephone 25882580.
Open 4pm. Rock, anything and everything.

LITERATURE

Literary life in Berlin is chaotic but fascinatingly so. More than
500 writers live in Berlin, about 200 earning their living by writing.
Some authors prefer to live some of the time in Berlin and some of
the time in West Germany, for example Günter Grass, whose
point of contact in Berlin is also as the President of the Akademie
der Künste. The atmosphere created by Berlin's tensions and contrasts, its often-mentioned and, by Berliners, not too infrequently
despaired-about 'island' position, the division of the former
capital, the old and new architecture, its political and symbolic
importance today and the history and tradition of literature still
apparent from pre-war Berlin are all obvious inspirations to both
writers and readers, but probably more than anything it is the
spirit created by people living in Berlin, their concerns, lifestyles
and interests, which sparks off a unique motivation to create and
enjoy literature.

Because most of the pre-war publishing houses have moved to
West Germany, Berlin is now the second city, after Munich, for
publishing, but the variety in methods of production does much to
compensate, ranging from the individually run back-street, hand-
press publisher to the larger more conventionally structured company. One could say that it is only to be expected of Berlin that a
small, independent, 'off' publisher might become more well-
known than a traditonal company.

Literary meeting-places, libraries and bookshops abound. The
bookshops are a book-worm's delight, stocking glorious stacks of
books displayed from floor to ceiling and offering years of rum-
maging. One of the reasons for the quality of the bookshops is the
centralised distribution system. 80% of all orders and deliveries
are made through one warehouse administered by the **Berliner
Verleger und Buchhändlervereinigung**, the Berlin Publishers' and
Booksellers' Union, Lützowstraß 105-106, 1000 Berlin 30,
Telephone: 262.1049/40. Deliveries are made daily and the following day's orders are collected at the same time.

Readings held in bookshops and galleries are a frequent and
important part of literary life in Berlin. The city centre has always
been a literary centre also; the pre-war bohemian-intellectual-
literary (for want of better words) cafe, the legendary Romanische

Café was situated on the present site of the Europa Center; the Buchhandlung Keller and the Autorenbuchhandlung renowned for their readings are both in Carmerstraße, not to mention the city bookshops and the **Literaturhaus** in Fasanenstraße which is the central city literary address.

Suitably set back from the city stress is the Literarisches Colloquium in Wansee, a meeting-place and literary centre for writers and film-makers, a centra often hosting the internationally renowned. Where one could describe the Literaturhaus as a place presenting literature to the public the Literarisches Colloquium serves as a place of inspiration for creators. Like Berlin!

MAJOR ADDRESSES

Literarisches Colloquium

The Literarisches Colloquium founded in 1963 as a centre for literature is the only one of its kind in West Germany. Since 1983 its work has been divided into three sections: literary events and programmes; photography and archives; film.

Its overall aim is to provide contact and means of discussion among writers, as well as theatre, film, television and radio writers and directors; to encourage literary life in West Berlin for itself and in the context of the other arts. Readings, seminars, courses, workshops, and discussion forums, often with the participation of famous international authors, are part of the programme. The Colloquium also works closely with the Akademie der Künste and the DAAD. It publishes the magazines 'Sprache im Technischen Zeitalter' and 'Literatur im Technischen Zeitalter' as well as publishing books and translating international literature into German.

The photography section is especially interested in photography's relation to literature, in book publishing for instance, and houses a comprehensive literary photo archive. The films produced by the Colloquium concentrate on literary themes and authors, or experimental forms.

Invited guests often stay at the guest house which is also open for 23.75 DM per night to those working in the arts or the media. Rooms can also be rented as studies. The setting, surrounded by trees and away from the hustle and bustle, is idyllic.
Sandwerder 5, 1000 Berlin 39, Telephone 8032082/8035681
President: Professor Harald Hartung
Administrative Director: Dr Wolfgang Trautwein.

Literaturhaus

Fasanenstraße 23, 1000 Berlin 15.

Opened in the Spring of 1986 as the central-city literary meeting place for writers, publishers, booksellers, librarians, academics, and generally where the lovers of literature can meet. The centre (most important!) a café **without** a closing time, three different rooms for readings, talks, discussions and multi-media programmes, a smaller more intimate room, the Tucholsky room, displaying the author's furniture and estate, a bookshop specialising in literature and apartments for invited guests.

Autorenbuchhandlung Berlin

Carmerstraße 10, 1000 Berlin 12, Telephone 2514015

The Autorenbuchhandlung, which opened in 1976, followed the Munich model of a bookshop created, financed and collectively administered by authors. Its aims are to encourage contemporary literature, to stock a complete selection of books by an author and books about an author and his or her works, and to build up the availability of specialist literature, for example political or avant garde literature, and poetry. The Autorenbuchhandlung (translated as Authors' Bookshop) is a major literary meeting-place in Berlin, holding readings, talks and discussions. There is usually a weekly programme on Tuesday evenings, for details phone the bookshop or refer to the published programme. Saturday, midday on, is also an informal time for writers and the interested to meet over coffee, to read and talk about their work. Not only is the Autorenbuchhandlung a first-class bookshop, it also stocks a good selection of literary and arts magazines.

Through the Autorenbuchhandlung one can also find out about the programme held in the **Buchhändlerkeller** a unique idea in Germany where rooms are set aside only for weekly readings. The address is Carmerstraße 1, 1000 Berlin 12, across the road from the Autorenbuchhandlung.

Forum unbekannter Autoren
Merseburger Straße 3, 1000 Berlin 62

A former Schöneberg factory, now converted into an art's centre with an 'alternative' atmosphere. Includes a gallery and writing and reading rooms and is a meeting-place for writers, musicians, artists, song-writers, actors and actresses.

Some other venues for readings, talks, discussions about literature.

Akademie der Künste, Hanseatenweg 10, 1000 Berlin 21, Telephone 391.1031.
Amerika Haus, Hardenbergstraße 22-24, 1000 Berlin 12, Telephone 819.7661.

Facades in Berlin — Steiglitz (mural Peter de Longueville)

British Centre, Hardenbergstraße 20, 1000 Berlin 12, Telephone 310.176.
Centre Francase de Wedding, Müllerstraße 74, 1000 Berlin 65
DAAD-Galerie, Kurfürstenstraße 58, 1000 Berlin 30, Telephone 261.3640
Cafe Einstein, Kurfürstenstraße 58, 1000 Berlin 30, Telephone 261.5096.
Elefanten Press Galerie, Zossener Straße 32, 1000 Berlin 61, Telephone 693.7026
Elwert und Meurer, Hauptstraße 101, 1000 Berlin 62, Telephone 784.001.
Europäischen Akademie Berlin, Bismarckallee 46, 1000 Berlin 33
Fabrik K 19 e.V., Klausener Platz 19, 1000 Berlin 19, Telephone 321.3435
Galerie am Chamissoplatz 6, 1000 Berlin 61, Telephone 692.5381/693.1891.
Haus am Kleistpark, Grunewaldstraße 6, 1000 Berlin 62, Telephone 342.2059
Haus am Lützowplatz, Lützowplatz 9, 1000 Berlin 30, Telephone 261.3805/261.4303.
Jüdische Gemeinde, Fasanenstraße 79-80, 1000 Berlin 19, Telephone 881.3538
Künstlerhaus Bethanien, Mariannenplatz 2, 1000 Berlin 36, Telephone 614.8010/614.9021
Literarischer Salon, Albrechtstraße 127, 1000 Berlin 41, Telephone 791.1187
Literaturcafe, Winterfeldstraße 36, 1000 Berlin 62.
Meta-Buchhandlung, Prinzregentenstraße 90, 1000 Berlin 31, Telephone 854.3216
Urania, Kleistraße 13-14, 1000 Berlin 30, Telephone 249.091
Wolff's Bücherei, Bundesallee 133, 1000 Berlin 41, Telephone 851.4264.

The Senate's encouragement of literature

As with all the arts, most of the financial support for literature is from the Senate and includes scholarships, prizes, financial help to authors, associations, publishers and centres such as the Literaturehaus in Fasanenstraße as well as the organising of international meetings and contacts among authors. The two literary prizes awarded by the Senate are:

Brüder-Grimm-Preis prize awarded for a dramatic work written for children or young people.

Moses-Mendelssohn-Preis awarded to a person, group or institution for an art work, or practical work achieved, conveying tolerance among peoples of different races, religions or world views.

Other prizes for literature:

Alfred-Döblin-Preis
c/o Akademie der Künste
Hanseatenweg 10,
1000 Berlin 21
Founded by Günter Gress for an unpublished work, about three-quarters completed.

Fontane Preis
c/o Akademie der Künste, as above.
The literature prize of the Academy's Kunstpreis Berlin awards.

Kritikerpreis
c/o Verband der Deutschen Kritiker e.V.
Cranachstraße 42,
1000 Berlin 41.
Critis' award to an author.

'Das Rote Tuch'
c/o Charlottenburg SPD
Otto-Shur-Allee 100,
1000 Berlin 10.
Prize awarded to a written work of any medium and suitable for those between 12 and 16 years which conveys criticism of fascism and the encouragement of democratic thought and action.

Private financial help for literature.

Hermann-Sudermann-Stiftung
Bettinastraße 3,
1000 Berlin 33.
Help to ill or needy authors.

Günter-Neumann-Stiftung
Schlüterstraße 36,
1000 Berlin 12.
Financial help for authors, composers, arrangers, actors/actresses, singers, readers in the fields of cabaret and comedy.

Wilhelm-Hauff-Preis
Schlüterstraße 49,
1000 Berlin 12.
Children's literature prize.

Institutions with sections on literature.

Akademie der Künste
Hanseatenweg 10,
1000 Berlin 21,
Telephone 391.1031.

Aspen Institut Berlin
Inselstraße 10,
1000 Berlin 38.
Telephone 803.9041.

Berliner Festspiele GmbH
Budapester Straße 50,
1000 Berlin 30,
Telephone 26341

Berliner Kulturat
Köthener Straße 44,

1000 Berlin 61.

Deutscher Akademischer Austauschdienst (DAAD)
Steinplatz 2,
1000 Berlin 12,
Telephone 31.04.61.

Deutsche Kultur-Gemeinschaft Urania Berlin e.V.
Kleiststraße 13-14,
1000 Berlin 30,
Telephone 2490/91.

Ibero-Amerikanisches Institut
Potsdamer Straße 37,
1000 Berlin 30,
Telephone 2665.

Künstlerhaus Bethanien
Mariannenplatz 2,
1000 Berlin 36.
Telephone 614.8010.

LITERARY ASSOCIATIONS

Adolf-Glaßbrenner-Gesellschaft: Europa-Center, 1000 Berlin 30.
Interest and encouragement of satire, especially works by Glaßbrenner and other Berlin satirists.

Abeitskreis Berliner Jungbuchhändler: Grolmannstraße 28, 1000 Berlin 12.
Free association for young booksellers. Organise readings in the Buchhändler-keller, held in Camerstraße 1, 1000 Berlin 12.

Arbeitskreis Literatur und Gesellschaft Freunde der Büchergilde: Kleistraße 19-21, 1000 Berlin 30.
Interest in literature in the context of the socio-political problems; literature and society. Organises readings.

Berliner Arbeitskreis Film: Schlüterstraße 53, 1000 Berlin 12.
Organises forums between film writers and others working in film, in the Literarisches Colloquim. (see also section on film).

Berliner Bibliophilen Abend: Marburger Staße 10, 1000 Berlin 30.
A society devoted to the care and quality of books.

Gehart-Hauptmann-Gesellschaft: Bismarckallee 14, 1000 Berlin 33.
Encouragement of Hauptmann's memory and works; care of the Hauptmann archive in the Staatsbibliothek.

Heinrich-von-Kleist-Gesellschaft: c/o Heinrich-von-Kleist-Gymnasium, Leuetzowstraße 3-5, 1000 Berlin 21.
Kleist's works read and discussed.

Literarische Werkstatt Kreuzberg: Solmsstraße 40, 1000 Berlin 61.
About 45 authors collect works by unknown authors for reading

and publication.

Max and Moritz-Gesellschaft: Berlepschstraße 60, 1000 Berlin 37. To encourage unknown authors in the fields of humour, satire and caricature. Scholarships, projects, helping authros, children's theatre, translation of 'Max und Moritz'.

Neue Gesellschaft für Literatur: e.V. Bismarckstraße 17, 1000 Berlin 12. Telephone 342.2059.
The major organisation in West Berlin for the overall encouragement of literary life in the city. Members include authors, readers, booksellers, critics etc. The association holds readings and forums. It also organises (with Kunstamt Schöneberg) the 'Lese Reihen' an annual literary programme/festival; and the autumn 'Berliner Autorentage' which has a different theme each year, each district's schools and libraries participating.
   The Neue Gesellschaft für Literatur is also an umbrella organisation for various workshops or smaller groups each with a specific function and interest.
For example: **Arbeitsgruppe Lyrik:** where authors read and discuss their poetry and publish anthologies.

Arbeitsgruppe Hörspiel/Feature: meetings of writers to read and discuss their radio-plays.

Arbeitsgruppe Literatur und Schule: a group with the aim of encouraging co-operation between authors and teachers. Authors are invited to schools, for example, and other programmes arranged.

Produktionsgruppe Mariannenpresse: serving the publishing house 'Edition Mariannenpresse' which publishes small runs of books combining literature and original graphics.

Arbeitsgruppe Tucholsky-Initiative: to maintain the birth-place of Tucholsky in Lübecker Straße 13.

Verein zur Föderung des Guten Jugendbuches: Wegenerstraße 6, 1000 Berlin 31.
Children's literature association.

Werkreis Literature der Arbeitswelt: Sondershauser Straße 75a, 1000 Berlin 46.
Seminars and readings.

Magazines and periodicals on literature and ideas.

Ästhetik und Kommunikation
Gneisenaustraße 2, im Mehringhof,
1000 Berlin 61.
Literature.

Das Argument
Altensteinstraße 48a
1000 Berlin 33.
Philosophy and social sciences.

europäische ideen
Postfach 246,
1000 Berlin 37.
Literature ideas.

Freibeuter
Bamberger Straße 6,
1000 Berlin 30.
Quarterly, cultural and political ideas.

Kursbuch
Potsdamer Straße 98,
1000 Berlin 30.
General.

L'80
Niedstraße 13,
1000 Berlin 41.
Literature and politics.

Literature im technischen Zeitalter
Am Sandwerder 5,
1000 Berlin 39.
Literature.

Litfass
Formerly a Berlin magazine, now based in Munich with a Berlin office: Stör Straße 19, 1000 Berlin 37.
Literature.

Neue Deutsche Hefte
Kindelbergweg 7,
1000 Berlin 46.

Sprache im Technischen Zeitalter
Am Sandwerder 5
1000 Berlin 39.

Stadtansichten
Kaiserdamm 27,
1000 Berlin 19.
Year book about literature and West Berlin cultural life.

Tintenfisch
Bamberger Straße 6,
1000 Berlin 30.
Year book of German literature.

Tumult
Berlin office: Pallas Straße 8,
1000 Berlin 30.

Smaller literary publications.

'Bekassine', 'Kernbeißer', 'Literatur und Erfahrung', 'Park', 'Silouette'

BOOKSHOPS

There are over 200 bookshops in West Berlin. The following
bookshops are specialist art bookshops or general bookshops
with large sections on the arts.

Autorenbuchlandlung,
Camerstraße 10,
1000 Berlin 12
Telephone 310151
Literature.

Buchhandlung am Savignyplatz
Savignyplatz 5,
Telephone 313.40.17
Was a centre for the '68 student rebellion. Politics, social

Bucherbogen, a Berlin bookshop

sciences, literature, theatre.

Bote und Bock
Hardenbergstraße 9a,
1000 Berlin 12,
Telephone 312.3081.
Books on music.

Bücherbogen
am Savignyplatz,
Stadbahnbogen 593,
1000 Berlin 12,
Telephone 312.1932.
The bookshop for architecture. Also art, design, photography, film, international catalogues, art magazines.

das europäische buch
Knesebeckstraße 3,
1000 Berlin 12,
Telephone 313.5056.
Branch: Thielallee 34,
Telephone 832.4051.
German literature, large selection from DDR.

Elwert und Meurer
Hauptstraße 101,
Telephone 784.001.
A general bookshop, comprehensive arts section.

Französische Buchhandlung
Libraire Francais
Kurfürstendamm 211,
Telephone 881.4156.

Galerie 2000
Knesebeckstraße 56-58,
1000 Berlin 15.
Telephone 883.8467.
Berlin's oldest art bookshop, enormous selection in all the fine arts as well as fashion, design, film, catalogues from wordwide, special and mail orders.

Gropius'che Buch und Kunsthandlung
Hohenzollerndamm 170,
1000 Berlin 31,
Telephone 860003-40.
Architecture and building construction.

Heinnrich Heine Buchhandlung
Im S-Bahnhof 200,
Telephone 313.4880
Especially good for literature, also art and music.

Kiepert KG
Hardenbergstraße 4-5,
Telephone 317031.

General; section on all the arts. Branch in Dahlem servicing the University, Garystraße 46,
Telephone 832.4368

Kommedia
Bundesallee 138,
Telephone 852.5910.
Bookshop specialising in the media, unique in Berlin.

Literatur-Kunst-Musik
Oranienstraße 21,
Telephone 652226.
Books on literature and music, exhibitions of art.

Pels Leusden Buchhandlung
Kurfürstendamm 59-60.
Telephone 323.2044/45.
Specialises in art books, especially painters and paintings. Also sections on literature and music.

Riedel
Uhlandstraße 38,
Telephone 882.7395.
Books on music.

Romanische Buchhandlung
Knesebeckstraße 18,
1000 Berlin 12,
Telephone 313.6905.
50% French literature; other half divided among Italian, Spanish and Portugese. Also magazines.

Marga Schoeller Bücherstube
Knesebeckstraße 33,
1000 Berlin 12.
Telephone 881.1112/22.
Before and during WW II reputedly the only bookshop in Berlin which refused to sell Nazi literature and somehow survived. It is **the** bookshop for books in English (70% of the stock) and books about film. Also theatre, music, ballet, Spanish and Italian literature, the humanities. Owned and run collectively.

Speth, Camilla, Buch und Kunsthandlung,
Kurfürstendamm 38/39,
Telephone 881.1545.
Art books and German literature.

Stodiecks
Richard-Wagner-Strabe 39,
1000 Berlin 10,
Telephone 31.1040.
Emigré literature, section on Polish literature, magazines, periodicals.

Wasmuth Buchhandlung
Hardenbergstraße 9a,

Telephone 316.920/313.8293.
Specialists in art history and architecture. Also antiquiriat.

Wolffs Bücherei
Bundesallee 133,
Telephone 851.4264.
Specialists in modern German literature.

Major Libraries

Staatsbibliothek
Potsdamer Straße 33, 1000 Berlin 30, Telephone 266-1.
Buses: 24,29,48,75,83.

The state city library of West Berlin, one of the largest in Europe, is housed in a building designed by Hans Scharoun. It serves as the most important scientific library for West Germany. Three to four million volumes, 32,000 current periodicals, handwritten scripts, musical scores, personal estates and autographs, maps, a picture archive, a lending section and reading room are all available for the public. As well as this there is a programme of concerts, lectures, discussions and exhibitions.

Kunstbibliothek
The Fine Arts Library
Jebensstraße 2, 1000 Berlin 12, Telephone 310116.
Open Monday and Thursday 1-7pm.
Tuesday, Wednesay, Friday 9-5pm.
Closed weekends.
Underground: Zoologische Garten

Apart from the 120,000 volumes and 630 periodicals available, the library also stores collections of prints, drawings and engravings, architectural drawings — worth mentioning is the collection of drawings and plans by architect Erich Mendelssohn — a poster

A Berlin bookshop

card collection (note the visiting cards) and a section on the history of book printing. Attached is the Lyperheide Costume Library, containing some 13,500 volumes and 46,000 prints showing examples of fashion and costume of different peoples at different times. The library is also a research or reading address and there are changing exhibitions.

More major libraries

Amerika-Gedenkbibliothek
Blücherplatz 1,
1000 Berlin 61.
Telephone 69050
Excellent arts' section

Freie Universität Berlin Universitätsbibliothek (University Library)
Garystraße 39,
1000 Berlin 33.
Telephone 838-1

Ibero-Amerikanisches Institut Bibliothek
Potsdamer Straße 37,
1000 Berlin 30.
Telephone 2665.
Latin, American, Spanish, Portugese literature and information.

Senatsbibliothek
Straße des 17 Juni 112,
1000 Berlin 12.
Telephone 31830

Technische Universität Berlin
Universitätsbibliothek (University Library)
Straße des 17 Juni 135,
1000 Berlin 12.
Telephone 3141
NOTE: Each district also has its own library.

Archives

Akademie der Künste (Archiv und Bibliothek
Archives and Library)
Hanseatenweg 10,
1000 Berlin 21.
Telephone 391.10.31

Archiv für Kunst und Geschichte
Archives for Art and History)
Teutonenstraße 221,
1000 Berlin 38.
Telephone 803.4054/5.

Bauhaus-Archiv
Klingelhöferstraße 14,
1000 Berlin 30.
Telephone 261.1618

Berlin Document Center,
Wasserkäfersteig 1,
1000 Berlin 37.
Telephone 819.7754

Bildarchiv Preußischer Kulturbesitz
Photo archives)
Hallesches Ufer 76,
1000 Berlin 61.
Telephone 266.2425/28.

Geheimes Staatsarchiv Preußischer Kulturbesitz
For historical information about Prussia)
Archistraße 12-14,
1000 Berlin 33.
Telephone 832031.

Landesarchiv Berlin
Kalckreuthstraße 12,
1000 Berlin 30.
Telephone 783.8586/80.

Landesbildstelle Berlin
Zentrum für audio-visuelle Medien
Audio-visual centre with Berlin film and photo Archives,
loaned out
Wilkingerufer 7,
1000 Berlin 21.
Telephone 390921

Rias Musikarchive
Music archives)
Kufsteiner Straße 69,
1000 Berlin 62.
Telephone 850.3435.

Sender Freies Berlin
Filmarchiv Fernsehen
(Film-television archives)
Masurenallee 8-14,
1000 Berlin 19.
Telephone 308.3000
Good material on the arts

Sender Freies Berlin
Hörfunkarchiv
(radio archives)
Masurenallee 8-14,
1000 Berlin 19.
Telephone 308-1
Good material on the arts.

Werkbund-Archiv
Schloßstraße 1a,
1000 Berlin 19.
Telephone 322.1061.

Documents and archives — see also section on galleries and institutions.

Publishers of books on the arts

Listed and described below are publishers who, usually among other books, publish books on the arts. 'Kunstlerbücher' refers to the publishing of books as an art form in itself, quite a feature of Berlin publishing.

Amsler und Ruthardt Nürnberger Straße 53, 1000 Berlin 30. Posters.

Ästhetik und Kommunikation Verlags, Gneisenaustraße 2 im Mehringhot, 1000 Berlin 61.
Autobiographies of artists.

Agora-Verlag, Manfred Schlösser Berlin-Darmstadt, Hanseatenweg 10, Postfach 210533, 1000 Berlin 21.
Unknown or forgotten works by young authors; emigré literature; music; poetry; the fine arts; literary criticism.

Albino Verlag, Postfach 620122, 1000 Berlin 62.
Literature, film, photography, painting.

Alphëus Verlag, Sigmaringer Straße 11, 1000 Berlin 31.
French literature; poetry and prose.

Alternative Verlag, Konstanzer Straße 11, 1000 Berlin 31.
Art and literary theory.

Anabis Verlag Sammlung Anabis, Markelstraße 1, 1000 Berlin 41.
The fine arts; Künstlerbücher.

arani-verlag, Kurfürstendamm, Postfach 310829, 1000 Berlin 31.
Poetry, Berlin.

Ararat Verlag, Kottbusser Damm 79, 1000 Berlin 61.
Literature; art postcards; Turkish culture; translations of Turkish literature into German.

Archibook Verlagsgesellschaft, Westendallee 97e, 1000 Berlin 19.
Architecture.

Verlag Willmuth Arenhövel, Treuchtlinger Straße 4, 1000 Berlin 30.
Architecture; arts and crafts.

Edition Ars Viva, Knesebeckstraße 76, 1000 Berlin 12.

Berliner Handpresse, Kohlfurter Straße 35, 1000 Berlin 36.
'Kunstlerbücher', small runs and original graphics; literature. Hand-press.

Berliner Verlagsbüro Han Günter Biel, Richard-Strauß-Straße 31, 1000 Berlin 33.
Literature.

Bote & Bock, Hardenbergstraße 9a, 1000 Berlin 12.
Contemporary music.

Burgent Handpresse Lassenstraße 22, 1000 Berlin 33.
Künstlerbücher, old poetry.

Verlag Ulrich Camen, Postfach 2921, 1000 Berlin 30.
Cultural history of eastern, southern and central eastern Europe.

Verlag das Europäische Buch, Thielallee 34, 1000 Berlin 33.
Knesebeckstraße 3, 1000 Berlin 12.
Fine arts and literature.

Deutscher Verlag für Kunstwissenschaft, Lindenstraße 76,
Postfach 110303, 1000 Berlin 61.
Art history and theory. Periodical for Deutschen Vereins für
Kunstwissenschaft.

Edition Neue Wege, Kaiserdamm 27, 1000 Berlin 19.
West Berlin authors.

Verlag Edition Orient, Grimmstraße 27, 1000 Berlin 61.
Arab prose and poetry. Books in Arabic and German.

Verlag Bernd Ehrig, Barstraße 28, 1000 Berlin 31.
Berlin; art catalogues; art books.

Elefanten Press Verlag, Zossener Straße 32, 1000 Berlin 61.
Catalogues; the fine arts, photography, film and television.

Express Edition, Kottbusser Damm 79, 1000 Berlin 61.
Literature of Turkish themes.

Wolfgang Fietkau Verlag, Potsdamer Chaussee 16, 1000 Berlin 37.
Contemporary authors.

Erika G. Freese, Potsdamer Straße 16, 1000 Berlin 45.
Clasical and modern literature; theatre; art history.

Friedenauer Press, Carmerstraße 10, 1000 Berlin 12.

Verlag Frölich und Kaufmann, Willdenowstraße 5, 1000 Berlin 65.
Fine arts; photography; architecture; cultural history; exhibition
catalogues.

Galerie/Edition Lietzow, Knesebeckstraße 32, 1000 Berlin 12.
Catalogues, drawings, original graphics.

Wabfer de Gruyter & Co, Berlin-New York, Genthiner Straße 12,
Postfach 110240, 1000 Berlin 30.
Literature; the fine arts; music.

Verlag Klaus Guhl Königin, Elisabeth-Straße 8, 1000 Berlin 19.
Exil-literature of the 1930's and 40's; film; the fine arts; modern
literature, 'Handbuch des Deutschen Theatres'.

Handpresse Gutsch, Am Vierrutenberg 47, 1000 Berlin 28.
Künstlerbücher. Hand-press, original graphics.

Marion Hildebrand Verlag, Gottschedstraße 2, 1000 Berlin 65.
Catalogues.

Verlag Hugo Hoffmann, Künstlerbücher.

Karl Junghans KG, Heesestraße 10, 1000 Berlin 41.
Handpress, original graphics.

Kiepert KG, Hardenbergstraße 4-5, 1000 Berlin 12.
Architecture.

Kluge und Morgenstern, Trabener Straße 39, 1000 Berlin 33.
Art painting and posters.

Konzert Verlag Gerhard Kowalski, Ringstraße 105, Postfach
450328, 1000 Berlin 45.
Music, jazz information, guides, handbooks etc.

Robert Lienau OHG, Lankwitzer Straße 9, 1000 Berlin 45.
Music and sheet music.

Edition Lindemann Otto Lindemann, Wiesbadener Straße 85, 1000
Berlin 41.
Music.

Liferanisches Colloquium Berlin, Am Sandwerder 5, 1000 Berlin
39.
Photography; prose; poetry; drama; essays; periodicals about
literature.

Gebr. Mann Verlag, Lindenstraße 76, Postfach 110303, 1000 Berlin
61.
Islamic art; art; cultural history; architecture and monuments.

Edition Mariannen Press, c/o Neue Gesellschaft für Literatur.
Bismarckstraße 17, 1000 Berlin 12.
Künstlerbücher — poetry/prose set with lithographs/linocuts.

Medusa Verlag, Körtestraße 18, 1000 Berlin 61.

Merve Verlag, Crellestraße 2, 1000 Berlin 62.
Avant-garde art.

Modular Verlag, Wiesbadener Straße 24, 1000 Berlin 33. Barstraße
8a, 1000 Berlin 31.
Music; the fine arts; poetry.

Redaktion 'Waage-Mut' Musculus Ritterstraße 95, 1000 Berlin 61.
Literature; music; caricature.

Nicolaische Verlagsbuchlandlung, Wilhelmsave 11, Postfach
31109, 1000 Berlin 31.
Photography; Berlin; art books.

Oberbaumuerlag Verlag für Literatur und Politik, Stromstraße 28, Postfach 127, 1000 Berlin 21.
Left wing literature; literature from black South Africa, Latin America, China.

Piratinnensender GBR, Wernigeroder Straße 11, 1000 Berlin 10.
Poetry; prose; women's literature.

Poll-edition, Lützowplatz 7, 1000 Berlin 30.
Catalogues; drawings; monographs.

Quadriga Verlag, Giesebrechtstraße 11, Postfach 125844, 1000 Berlin 12.
Architecture, theatre.

Rainer Verlag, Körtestraße 10, 1000 Berlin 61.
Künstlerbücher, modern literature and art.

Dietrich Reimer Verlag, Unten den Eichen 57, 1000 Berlin 45.
Catalogues.

Rembrandt Verlag, Schaperstraße 35, 1000 Berlin 15.
Fine arts; music; theatre; dance; film.

Rotbuch Verlag, Potsdamer Straße 98, 1000 Berlin 30.
Literature; the periodical "Frauen und Film".

Fachverlag Schiele & Schön, Markgrafenstraße 11, 1000 Berlin 61.
Photography; video film.

Harald Schmid Edition Pegasus, Röntgenstraße 7, 1000 Berlin 10.
Poetry, novels, prose.

Wilhelm Schneider & Co., Feurigstraße 54, 1000 Berlin 62.
Engravings, etchings, reproductions of paintings.

Richard Seitz & Co., Pätzer Straße 11, 1000 Berlin 47.
Art; Berlin literature.

Siedler Verlag, Giesebrechtstraße 11, Postfach 125844, 1000 Berlin 12.
Literature; art history.

Verlag Volker Spiess, Großgörschenstraße 6, Postfach 147, 1000 Berlin 62.
Film & media periodicals.

Stattbuch Verlag, Greisenaustraße 2, 1000 Berlin 19.
Annual handbook about 'alternative' Berlin.

Stroemfeld/Roter Stern, Sedingstraße 47, 1000 Berlin 19.
Literature.

Transit Buchverlag, Greisenaustraße 2, 1000 Berlin 61.
Literature.

Verlag Ullstein, Lindenstraße 76, Postfach 110303, 1000 Berlin 61.
Literature.
Part of Ullstein is **Propyläen Verlag**, publishing the classics; art books; art history; books about literature.

Verlag Klaus Wagenbach, Bamberger Straße 6, Postfach 1409, 1000 Berlin 30.
Literature.

THEATRE

There are three groups or types of theatres in West Berlin, loosely termed 'state', 'private', and 'free'. State theatres are fully financed by the Berlin Senate. There are three such theatres: Schiller-Theatre and the Schiller-Theatre Werkstatt, Schloßpark-Theatre and Theatre des Westens.

The Schiller-Theatre and Werkstatt and the Schloßpark Theatre each receive annually about 32 million DM. The Theatre des Westens, a theatre specialising in musicals and operettas, received 12-13 million DM annually. The theatres are run autonomously and each is independent of the others. There is no pressure to be either popular or commercial. The state theatres present the best of world drama, the classics of past and present German drama, or international choices ranging from ancient Greek drama to contemporary English, French or American drama.

Some private theatres also receive financial assistance; Schaubühne am Lehniner Platz, for example, received around 14 million DM, the Freie Volksbühne about four and a half million DM and the Renaissance Theatre around three million DM. There are two main differences between the state and private-subsidised theatres with regard to their budgets, firstly, that the latter are financed both by subsidy and by bookings; secondly, that the state theatres are allotted money for specific departments (for example, so much for wardrobe, so much for salaries etc) while the subsidised theatres are free to allot as they please. Subsidised theatres argue that this allows more room for experiment and that with the protection of a subsidy they enjoy the best of both worlds.

Other theatres, for example the boulevard theatres Komödie, Theater am Kurfurstendamm or the Hansa Theater are privately owned and run commercially and are not subsidised.

The 'free' or 'off' groups have been an important part of Berlin theatre life for the last decade or so. They are usually non-traditional, experimental groups created by professionals or amateurs — mainly young artists. They cannot be identified with particular theatres and perform in a variety of places, for example, traditional theatres, old picture theatres, factories, halls or studios. The 'free' groups do not receive an annual grant or subsidy but the Senate does support individual productions. Three interesting names to watch out for at present art: Theatermanufaktur, Transformtheater, and Rote Grütze, a children's and young people's theatre.

The Deutsche Oper
Bismarckstraße 35, 1000 Berlin 10, Telephone 343.81.

The Deutsche Oper Berlin opened in Bismarckstraße in 1961 on the site where the Charlottenburg Deutches Opernhaus had stood from 1912 until 1943. After the war the Oper's home (known as the Städtische Oper) was the Theater des Westens in Kantstraße

Since 1981 the company has been directed by Professor Götz Friedrich and its musical director Dr Jesus Löpez Cobos. The company's repertoire is wide; including 60 operas and 40 ballets in repertory, combining the favourites with the less known. This variety is exemplified by the 1984-85 seasn which included works by Beethoven, Berg, Debussy, Donizetti, Handel Humperdinck, Kelterborn, Mozart, Mussorgsky, Offenbach, Puccini, Reimann, Rihm, Verdi and Wagner, among many others.

As well as opera and ballet smaller-scale works are also presented, for instance lieder evenings, (1984-5 soloists included Janet Baker, Simon Estes, Dietrich Fischer-Dieskau, Montserrat Caballé, Brigitte Fassbender, Luciano Pavarotti) concerts, chamber music, midnight medleys in the foyer, films, discussions and special performances for young people.

The Deutsche Oper in Bismarckstraße was designed by Hans Bornemann. The auditorium seats 1900.

A 'Friends of the Deutsche Oper' association helps support the opera company and house; for information contact the above address and telephone number.

State Theatres

Schloßpark Theater

Scloßstraße 48,
1000 Berlin 41.
Telephone 31951.
Box Office: 791.1213.
Underground: Rathaus Steglitz.
Box Office open from 10am
Repertoire: Classical, contemporary, at times experimental.

Schiller-theater

Bismarckstraße 110,
1000 Berlin 12.
Telephone 31951.
Underground: Ernst-Reuter-Platz.
Box Office open from 10am.
Repertoire: Classical and contemporary.

Schiller-Theater Werkstatt

Address as above. Studio theatre; seating around 150 depending upon production. Repertoire: experimental.

Theater des Westens

Kantstaße 12,
1000 Berlin 12.
Telephone 310685/9
Underground: Zoologische Garten

Box Office 3121022/3125015
From 10am to 6pm
Sundays and holidays 3pm to 6pm.
Repertoire: A theatre for musicals and operettas.

General Drector of all the state theatres: Heribert Sasse.
Artistic Director: Dr.Gerhard Blasche.

Private Theatres

Schaubühne am Lehniner Platz.
Kurfürstendamm 153,
1000 Berlin 31.
Telephone 89 00 20
Box Office 89 00 23,
Underground: Adenauer Platz
Bookings 10am-7pm.
Sunday and holidays 10am-2pm and after 5pm.

This is the most significant theatre in West Berlin today and certainly one of this century's most important theatres. Peter Stein as artistic director ranks as one of the greats with Reinhardt or Stanislavsky. It was founded in 1962 as Schaubühne am Halleschen Ufer by Leni Langenscheidt, Waltraud Mau, Jürgen Schitthelm and Klaus Weiffenbach and since that time has been collectively run.

The repertoire is wide, including both German and international drama. Despite the company's being influenced by the student movement of the late sixties-early seventies andits beginnings as an 'off' theatre, there is no ideological criteria in choosing a work, simply that a play is of quality and that it inspires thought about contemporary personal and public problems and feelings. Another important artistic decision is that the text is respected and the play represented in its own time or the time of writing.

Plays are chosen by the whole company including technical

The Schaubuhne, one of Berlin's top theatres

staff; the company is open, democratic and a collective. This works because the company is relatively small, comprising of about 25-30 actors and actresses plus 20 additional personel, also because many have worked together for years and know deeply the qualities of each other and not least because of the outstanding talent in the company itself which has served as continuous inspiration and motivation.

One of the refreshing aspects of the Schaubühne is that its fame was created by the quality of the performances themselves. Publicity is word of mouth — there are no press or publicity departments, no advertising campaigns, no season's bookings. Nothing is 'jacked up'. Premiere dates are left open; the play opens when it is artistically ready. Quality first: it has worked!

Freie Volksbühne Berlin
Schaperstraße 24,
1000 Berlin 15.
Telephone 8842080
Underground: Spichernstraße
Box Office 8813742
Pre-bookings 10am-2pm and one hour before the performance.
The Freie Volksbühne was created by the Social Democrats in 1890 to enable and encourage workers to see more theatre. In the 1890's it performed works by Ibsen and Hauptmann, among others. Today there is no fixed company and the repertoire is open. The new building, seating 1017, opened in 1963. It is an influential theatre in Berlin of high reputation. The general and artistic director is Kurt Hübner.

Grips Theater
Altonaer Straße 22,
1000 Berlin 21,
Telephone 3933012
Underground: Hansaplatz
Box Office Telephone 3914004.
Actors in the Grips Theater also write their own plays, some of which have been performed world-wide. The theatre has had a tremendous influence in Berlin and is now subsidised by the Senate.

Hansa Theater
Alt Moabit 48,
1000 Berlin 21.
Telephone 3927377.
Underground: Turmstraße.
Pre-bookings 10-7pm, Sunday 3-6.
A smallish theatre opened in 1963 under the directorship of Paul Esser and from 1981 directed by Horst Nierendorf. Known as Berliner Volkstheater its repertoire is middle-brow.

Hebbel Theater
Sresemannstraße 29,
1000 Berlin 61.
Telephone 2512773.
Opened in 1909 with Hebbel's 'Maria Magdalene'. It is at present being renovated and its place in Berlin's theatre life undecided.

Kleines Theater
Südwestkorso 64,
1000 Berlin 41.
Telephone 821.2021.Underground: Friedrich-Wilhelm-Platz
Bookings 11-5, also by telephone. Box Office on days of perfor-
mance open from 6-8pm.
A small experimental theatre and cabaret. Seats 99. Director
Sabine Fromm. Artistic Director Pierre Baden.

Komödie
Kurfürstendamm 206/7,
1000 Berlin 15.
Telephone 8827893.
Underground: Uhlandstraße
Pre-bookings 10-7, Sunday 3-7.
A 'boulevard theatre' commercially run. Performs mainly
American, English or French works. Opened in 1924 with the
legendary Max Reinhardt as director. Present direction under:
Knut Lehmann, Wolfgang Spier, Jürgen Wölffer, Christian Wölf-
fer.

Renaissance-Theater
Hardenbergstaße 6,
1000 Berlin
Telephone 3124202
Underground: Ernst-Reuter-Platz
Box Office 10.30-8pm
Sunday 3.30-8pm.
A wide repertoire, performing both the boulevard-Broadway style
play and the more literary.

Theater am Kurfürstendam.
Kurfürstendamm 209,
1000 Berlin 15,
Telephone 8813020.
Underground: Uhlandstraße.
Box Office 8812489.
Bookings 10-7, Sunday 3-6.
Build in 1921, rebuilt after the war and reopened in 1963 under
Hans Wölffer, who owns this theater and Komödie. Like the latter
it is also a 'boulevard theatre' performing mainly American,
English or French drama.

Tribune,
Otto-Suhr-Allee 18-20,
1000 Berlin 10
Telephone 3419001
Underground: Ernst-Reuter-Platz..
Box Office 3412600
Bookings Monday 2-6, Tuesday-Sunday 2-7.
Like the Renaissance Theater, Tribune performs a wide variety of
plays from the Broadway hits to the more 'intellectual'. Not a fix-
ed company. Director Klaus Sonenschein.

Vaganten Bühne Berlin
Kantstraße 12a,

Tent of Fringe theatre Tempodrom

1000 Berlin 12,
Telephone 3124529.
Underground Zoologische Garten.
Box Office 3124529.
Bookings Monday 10-5, Tuesday-Friday 10-7, Saturday and Sunday 5-7.
Small experimental cellar theatre. Seating 100. Director Rainer Behrend.

'Off' Theatres

The six most renowned during the 1984-5 season were:
Jung Ensemble für Musiktheater
Rote Grütze
Tanzfabrik (dance-drama, see also section on dance).
Theater zum Westlichen Staathirchen.
Transformtheater.
Theatermanufaktur am Helleschen Ufer.

Other groups to look out for are:
T.I.A.S.
Theater am Kreuzberg
Theater Francais
Tigertheater
Junges Theater
Mehringhotheater

Useful information

Drama Schools

The drama section at the **Hochschule der Künste,** Fasanenstraße 1, telephone 31850, is the best tuition for the theatre overall. Also taught are theatre history, dance and costume.

The Schaubühne plans in 1986 to select 4-5 young actors/actresses for the first pupils in their small theatre school. The course will be for three years and only when the first group have finished will the next five be chosen, (not a semester system). Part of the training will be working in the theatre itself.

Private drama schools.
The best private school for professionals is **Der Kreis: Fritz-Kirchhoff Schule,** founded in 1945, in Glogaoer 6, 1000 Berlin 36. Telephone 618.5948.

Other private schools are:
Jürgen von Alten Schauspielstudio, Hartmannstraße 17, Telephone 771.8463.
Marie Luise Anger, Meiningenal 15, 1000 Berlin 19, Telephone 304.3575.
Schauspielstudio und Film Atelier Langhanke, Seehofstraße 24, 1000 Berlin 37, Telephone 811.1385.

Magazines: There is no specifically Berlin theatre magazine but the best magazine about the theatre in Germany is based in Berlin and is entitled **'Theater Heute'**, Lützowplatz 7, 1000 Berlin 30, Telephone 261.7003.

Also of interest for further information is the recently published and most comprehensive guide to the theatre life in Berlin called **Theaterbuch Berlin.** Written by Jürgen Hoffmann and published by Verlag Klaus Guhl. The same publishers also publish the **Handbuch des Deutschen Theaters.**

Theatre Critics.
Friedrich Luft, a critic now for fifty or so years, the most notable and influential in Berlin and well-known throughout Germany. Writes for 'Welt' and 'Morgenpost'.
  Herr Kotshenreuther writes for 'Der Tagespiegel', Rainer Schweinfurth for 'Zitty' and Rüdiger Schaper for 'Tip'. Another very interesting critic with an original analytical approach is Andreas Rossmann.

Prizes

Brüder Grimm Preis: Awarded for the best children's play written in German, chosen by jury. Every two yeas. Prize worth 10,000 DM.
Gerhard Hauptmann Prize, given by the Freie Volksbühne to an author writing in the German language.
The **Kunstpreis** might be awarded to an actor/actress, and the **Critics Prizes** are also awarded for theatre.

Grants and scholarships: there are DAAD scholarships for overseas as well as grants given by the Akademie der Künste.

Bookshops Marga Schoeller in Knesebeckstraße, Bücherbogen on Savigny Platz, Kommedia in Bundesallee. Also Galerie 2000 in Knesebeckstraße for books on costume design.

Useful Addresses
Genossenschaft Deutscher Bühnen-Angehörigen, Joachim-Friedrich-Strasse 54, Telephone 892.9493. This is the union for all

performing artists.

International Theatre Institut — Germany
Bismarckstraße 17, 1000 Berlin 12, Telephone 341.8010.

Besucher Organisations There are four theatre Besucher organisations in Berlin. They sell season's tickets at a cheaper rate, usually ten performances are included. In West Berlin the total number of people belonging to such organisations is around 100,000.

Theatergemeinde is the largest with over 30,000 members, the Freie Volksbühne and the Berliner Theater-Club next, each with about 25,000 members, and the smallest, with 5000 members, the Berliner Besucher Ring (und Theater Schulen).

Festivals: Theatertreffen, part of the annual festivals organised by the Berliner Festspiele. See section on festivals.

DANCE

Perhaps because ballet was never focussed upon in Berlin compared with the other arts, there was more room for the flourishing of new dance forms. Isadora Duncan, for instance, opened her first school in Grunewald and Rudolf von Laban's and Mary Wigman's contributions influenced not only their contemporaries in Berlin but dancers throughout the world. This feeling for exploration in dance has again struck Berlin with the formation of companies like Tanzfabrik, Tanz Tangenta and Central Park. The one ballet company in Berlin is attached to the Deutsche Oper.

Dance Companies and Schools

Ballet-Akademie Hans Vogl

Atl Moabit 48, 1000 Berlin 21, Telephone 3914106. Ballet school.

Barbara Heinisch during a paint performance

Balletschule Anita Barth

Ruhrstraße 12a, 1000 Berlin 31, Telephone 877720. Ballet school.

Berliner Tanzakademie

Grainauerstraße 12, 1000 Berlin 30, Telephone 2131699. This is the ballet school of the Deutsche Oper Ballet Company, which is the one professional ballet company in Berlin.

Die Etage

Hasenheide 54, 1000 Berlin 61, Telephone 6912095. A school teaching a wide range of movement including different dance forms, acrobatics, pantomime and drama. The school offers a three year tuition to professional standard. Shorter courses are also held in most forms of dance.

Central Park

Windscheidstraße 18, 1000 Berlin 12, Telephone 323.7082. Performing company and school. Chief choreographer: Regina Baumgart. School and courses in ballet, modern jazz, step, improvisation.

Russische Balletschule Lydia Wolgina

Hauptstraße 78/79, 1000 Berlin 41, Telephone 8520694/7850189. Russian ballet school of Lydia Wolgina.

Studio Olivier Pascalin

Lepsiusstraße 14, 1000 Berlin 14, Telephone 7916190/7913395. Workshops and courses in different forms of dance for amateurs and professionals. Courses also for fashion models, actors and actresses.

Tanzfabrik e.V.

Möckernstraße 68, 1000 Berlin 61, Telephone 7865861. This company, formed as a collective in 1978, has become the most renowned experimental dance company in Germany, and well-known throughout Europe. Its repertoire is created by choreographers and from improvisation to live or recorded music or speech. The focus is on modern dance, dance-theatre and experimental dance forms. The company has performed at many international festivals and has toured extensively. In 1980 it received a Kulturpreis des. Tanzfabrik also runs a school which teaches modern, jazz, contact, improvisation ballet, tai chi, performance and dance for children.

Tanz Tangente

Kuhligkshofstraße 4, 1000 Berlin 41, Telephone 7929124. This is also a performing company and school. The company performs a mixture of American influenced modern and jazz techniques;

chief choreographer Leonora Ickstadt. Influences of Graham and Wigman, for example. The school offers courses in modern, jazz, improvisation and creative dance for children.

FILM

Most of the films shown in Berlin straight after the war were from Hollywood, or were commercial French or English films, and the University Film Clubs were the only significant centres showing the more thought-provoking, or 'art' films. In 1963 the Berlin University Film Club formed the Freunde der Deutschen Kinemathek which laid the basis for an alternative to the weighty dose of post-war escapism. Showings were held in the Akademie der Künste as well as a variety of Berlin picture theatres and included retrospectives, experimental and avant garde films.

'Arsenal', founded in 1970 by the Freunde der Deutschen Kinemathek, was the first and is still the most important 'Off Kino' in Berlin. Its repertoire is as wide as film-making itself, showing films from 1895 to the present; Hollywood to the most way-out experimental (including video and Super 8); political documentaries; retrospectives; films not only from the West but also the Eastern block and the Third World. 'Arsenal' was the springboard for the development of 'Off Kinos' not only in Berlin but throughout the Bundesrepublik, and internationally, though not as large or as flash as the National Film Theatre in London, its importance is comparable. There are three showings weekdays and four showings on both Saturday and Sunday. Each time one enters 'Arsenal' one is struck again by its special atmosphere, difficult to to describe precisely because it conveys that peculiarly deep combination of mystery and intimacy that films at their best also create.

'Arsenal' publishes its own programme and the programme for most of the 'Off Kinos' are published in 'filmszene', which is free and can be found in all the 'Off Kinos'. They are listed below:

'Off Kinos'

Arsenal

Welserstraße 25, 1000 Berlin 30, Telephone 246848.
Underground: Wittenbergplatz/Viktoria-Luise-Platz.
Buses: 19,29,60,73,85.

Babylon

Dresdnerstraße 126, 1000 Berlin 36, Telephone 614.6316
Underground: Kottbusser Tor, bus 28.

Bali

Teltower Damm 33, 1000 Berlin 31, Telephone 8114678
Underground: S-Bahn Zehlendorf.

Broadway

Tauentzienstraße 8, 1000 Berlin 30, Telephone 261.5074.
Underground: Wittenbergplatz, Buses: 19,29.

Cinema

Bundesallee 111, 1000 Berlin 41, Telephone 852.3004
Underground: Walter-Schreiber-Platz
Buses: 2,17,30,48,75,76,85,90.

Filmbühne am Steinplatz

Hardenbergstraße 12, 1000 Berlin 12, Telephone 312.9012.
Underground: Zoologische Garten.
Buses: 23,54,262,73,90,92,94.
Also has a cafe-restaurant to sit, eat, talk, read. . .

Filmkunst 66,

Bleibtreustraße 12, 1000 Berlin 12, Telephone 881.5510
Underground: Uhlandstraße, Buses: 9,19,29,92,94.

Graffiti

Parisier Straße 44, 1000 Berlin 15, Telephone 883.4335
Buses: 60,69,89.

Hollywood

Kurfürstendamm 65, 1000 Berlin 15, Telephone 883.5077
Underground: Adenauerplatz, buses: 9,19,29,74.
Only some programmes 'off'.

Kant-Kino

Kantstraße 54, 1000 Berlin 12, Telephone 312.5047
Underground: Wilmersdorferstraße, buses: 1,66,92,94.

Kid

Part of Kant-Kino above

Klick

Windscheidstraße 19, 1000 Berlin 12, Telephone 323 8437, Buses:
10,21,66,74,82,84.

Die Kurbel

Giesebrechtstraße 4, 1000 Berlin 12, Telephone 883.5325

Underground: Adenauerplatz
Buses. 1,9,19,29,69,74.

Lupe 1

Kurfürstendamm 202, 1000 Berlin 15, Telephone 883.6106.
Underground: Uhlandstraße
Buses: 9,19,29,60.

Lupe 2

Olivaer Platz 15, 1000 Berlin 15, Telephone 881.1170
Buses: 1,9,19,29,60.

Manhattan

Wilhelmsruher Damm 128, 1000 Berlin 26, Telephone 415.9000
Buses: 21,22,62,64.

New-York

Yorckstraße 86, 1000 Berlin 61, Telephone 786.5070
Underground: Mehringdamm, Buses: 19,28.

Notausgang

Vorbergstraße 1, 1000 Berlin 62, Telephone 781.2682
Underground: Kleistpark.
Buses 4,48,75,83,84.

Studio

Kurfürstedamm 71, 1000 Berlin 31, Telephone 3245003
Underground: Adenauerplatz, Buses: 9,10,19,29,69.

Sylvia

Hauptstraße 116, 1000 Berlin 62, Telephone 7815667
Underground: Rathaus Schöneberg,
Buses: 4,48,83,84.

Note also:

Capitol Dahlem, the oldest student picture theatre.
Thielallee 36, 1000 Berlin 33, Telephone 832.8527
Underground: Thielplatz

and:

Ufer Palast/UFA Fabrik

Viktoriastraße 13, 1000 Berlin 42, Telephone 752.6078
Underground: Ullsteinstraße, Buses: 25,68

Important Film Addresses

Akademie der Künste

Hanseatenweg 10,
1000 Berlin 21,
Telephone 391.1031.

Arsenal
Freunde der Deutsche Kinematek

Welserstraße 25,
1000 Berlin 30,
Telephone 24.68.48/213.6030

Berliner Arbeitskreis Film,

Schlüterstraße 53,
1000 Berlin 12.
Telephone 881.8555, mornings only.
An organisation devoted to the integration of film-making and connected interests. It arranges discussions for instance, and contacts among writers and directors and works with the Literarisches Colloquium (see also literature section).

Club der Filmjaumalisten Berlin e.V

Dernburgstraße 57,
1000 Berlin 19.
Telephone 321.7977

DAAD film section

Steinplatz 2,
1000 Berlin 2.
Telephone 31.04.61.

Deutsche Film und Fernsehakademie Berlin School teaching film and television direction; camerawork.
Deutsche Kinemathek (archive of films and film photos).
Pommernallee 1,
1000 Berlin 19.
Telephone 30.36.1

Internationale Filmfestspiele

Berlin's international and renowned film festival, which also includes the festival of experimental and avant garde films. **'internationales forum des jungen films'** which received the Kritikverbandes FIPRESCI prize in 1971 and the Berlin Kunst Prize in 1973. Both festivals part of Berliner Festpiele
Budapester Straße 48/50.
1000 Berlin 30.
Telephone 26.34.1

Literarisches Colloquium Berlin,

Am Sandwerder 5

1000 Berlin 39.
Telephone 803.56.81.
Also has a film section; organises contacts between writers and
film-makers; makes films on literary themes.

Der Senator für Kulturelle Angelegenheiten

Europa Center
1000 Berlin 30.
Telephone 21.23.3200

Verband der Filmarbeiterinnen

Apostel-Paulus-Straße 32,
1000 Berlin 62.
Telephone 781.78.92/341.20.13
Association for women working with film.

The Ruins of the Anhalter Bahnhof, a former railway station

For the best selection of books on film:
Marge Schoeller Bücherstube
Knesebeckstr 33/34.
Telephone 811.11.12
and the best library for books on film:
Bibliothek des Deutschen Film und Fernsehakademie Berlin
Pommernallee 1,
1000 Berlin 19.
Telephone 30.36.1
Note: A film centre housing all the main film addresses under one roof is planned for the future, to be called Esplanade.

ARTS FESTIVALS

The major festivals held in Berlin are organised by a corporation called Berliner Festspiele, housed in Budapester Strasse 50, 1000 Berlin 30, Telephone 26341. The festivals are listed below, in order of their occurence in the year.

Internationale Filmfestspiele Berlin — International Film Festival

This is an internationally renowned festival, usually held in February, attracting, among the interested, top film-makers from abroad. A different theme provides a focus each year. As well as the enormous variety of international films screened, less-known films, children's films, films shown to buyers, are also part of the festival. A workshop festival for experimental and avant-garde films, the **Internationales Forum des Jungen Filmes**, is an added highlight. The awarding of the gold and silver 'Berliner Bären' climaxes the film festival.

Theatertreffen Berlin — Berlin Theatre Meeting

A Spring Festival usually held in May where German-speaking companies are invited to show their best pieces of the past year. The meeting is a forum for theatre people. critics and the public to enjoy, discuss, compare, learn and make contacts, and it is now considered the most important drama festival for German-speaking theatre. At the end of the festival a **Schüler-Theatertreffen**, a school drama festival, is held, where groups are invited from West Germany to perform in Berlin.

Berlin Festwochen · Berlin Festival Weeks

This is the main Berlin arts' festival and Berlin festival, held in Autumn, September-October, combining programmes of music, theatre, dance, literary events and fine arts exhibitions. A different theme chosen for each festival gives orientation to the weeks of fantastic variety. A test of any festival must ultimately be the public's response: in 1984, 95% of seats were sold!

Jazzfest Berlin

A November festival well-placed to defuse the first shudders of winter. The Jazz festival offers international 'stars' and a place

where the latest sounds can be heard. Experimental juxtapositions such as jazz and symphonic or non-European music also feature.
The **Total Music Meeting** of free European jazz musicians runs parallel to the festival.

Horizonte — Horizons

All the festivals have in common their aim of strengthening international contact and to emphasise this further a festival of non-European cultures is organised every few years. For each such festival a different culture or part of the world is chosen as an overall theme and a myriad of exhibitions, performances, forums and workshops are offered. To spoil the Berliner and visitor to Berlin even further the different arts each have their own festivals. There is, for instance, the fine arts festival **Kunst Konzentriert** where a number of galleries show special exhibitions and are open on several days for longer hours (organised by the Interressengemeinschaft Berliner Kunsthändler e.V, Ludwigkirchstraße 11a, 1000 Berlin 15, Telephone 883.2643). One should also note the annual **Freie Berliner Kunstaustellung** held usually in the Spring, an enormous art exhibition showing works by Berlin artists.
Ex Libris Berliner Bücherforum is a literature festival organised by the Neue Gesellschaft für Literatur e.V. (The New Literature Association) and the Arbeitsgemeinschaft Kleinerer Verlage in der BVG (small publishers association).

Note: See music section for further music festivals.

INTERNATIONAL CULTURAL CENTRES AND CONSULATES

Amerika Haus: Hardenbergstraße 22/24, 1000 Berlin 12, Telephone 819.7661.
Library; music (mainly jazz); exhibitions; film; discussions and lectures. All presentations have some connection with the United States. Academic scholarships for students to study in the United States are available. Programmes and scholarships for artists of German nationality for further study in the U.S. are organised through the DAAD or the Berlin Senate.

Aspen Institute Berlin: Inselstraße 10, 1000 Berlin 38, Telephone 803.9041.
This centre has the distinction of being the only Aspen Institute outside of the United States. Holds lectures on humanistic studies.

The British Council: The British Centre Berlin, Hardenbergstraße 20, 1000 Berlin 12, Telephone 310176.
The British Centre's programme includes films; concerts (mainly chamber, jazz or folk); theatre, including fringe theatre; and lectures. The library contains 19,500 titles, entirely British. A wide selection of up-to-date British magazines, periodicals and newspapers are also available.
    The British Centre also encourages contact between Berlin and Britain through academic, educational and artistic exchanges,

The Coachman's House, an exhibition venue in Kreuzberg

scholarships, bursaries, visitorships, group study tours, academic travel grants, summer school courses and conversation classes.

Institute Francais de Berlin: Kurfürstendamm 211, 1000 Berlin 15, Telephone 8818702.
Library and reading room. Films; exhibitions; lectures; courses; language tuition.

Centre Francais Berlin: Müllerstraße 74, 1000 Berlin 65, Telephone 418.1418/418.766

Europäische Akademie Berlin: Bismarckallee 46/48, 1000 Berlin 33, Telephone 826.2095.

Jüdische Volkshochschule Berlin: Fasanenstraße 79-80, 1000 Berlin 12, Telephone 88420336
Part of the Jewish Community Centre's activities offering a range of lectures and discussions on subjects including art, literature, general humanistic studies and other topics. See published programme.

Kurdisches Kultur und Beratungzentrum, Kolonnenstraße 47, 1000 Berlin 62, Telephone 782.1170.

Lessing Hochschule: Hardenbergstraße 7, 1000 Berlin 12, Telephone 3129007/3139607.
Lectures on a wide range of topics including the fine arts, music and literature. See published programme.

Türkenzentrum: Schinkel Straße 8/9,1000 Berlin 44, Telephone 6911028.

Urania Berlin-Deutsche Kultur-Gemeinschaft: Kleiststraße 13,

1000 Berlin 30, Telephone 249.091.
Holds discussions, lectures, forums to further international cultural information; literary events, music, exhibitions.

Consulates

Amerikanisches Generalkonsulat
Clayallee 170, 1000 Berlin 33, Telephone 819.7459/819.7450

Britisches Generalkonsulat
Uhlandstraße 7/8, 1000 Berlin 12, Telephone 309.5293.

Französisches Generalkonsulat
Kurfürstendamm 211, 1000 Berlin 15, Telephone 881.8028/29.

Generalkonsulate der UdSSr in den Westsektoren Berlins
Reichensteiner Weg 34/36, 1000 Berlin 33, Telephone 832.7004/5.

Italienisches Generalkonsulat
Graf-Spree-Straße 1/7, 1000 Berlin 30, Telephone 2611591/92/93.

Türkisches Generalkonsulat
Johann-Georg-Straße 11 & 12, 1000 Berlin 31, Telephone 892.5033/34.

'OFF CENTRES'

'Off-centres', as they are termed in Berlin, are art centres and meeting-places which are usually non-profit collectives. They are 'alternative' in the sense that they believe that the arts should be created rather than consumed, tasted rather than swallowed. The centres are sometimes meeting-places and even homes as well as places to perform or exhibit. Because new centres are continually opening and established centres closing it's best to refer to the latest copies of 'Tip', 'Zitty', or 'Statbuch' for names and addresses. At present two important centres are Tempodrom and Ufa Fabrik.

GENERAL INFORMATION

TOURIST INFORMATION

The most useful address for all tourist information as well as accommodation advice is the **Verkehrsamt Berlin**, the Berlin Tourist Information Office. This is in the Europa Center (Budapester Straße entrance), Telephone 262.6031. Open daily from 7.30am-10.30pm.

The Informationzentrum Berlin, The Berlin Information Centre, is in Hardenbergstraße 20, 1000 Berlin 12, and is the central office for all general information about Berlin — facts and figures and so forth. It also organises programmes for young people's groups visiting Berlin and gives advice about hostel accommodation. The telephone number is 31.00.40 and it is open Monday — Friday from 8am-7pm, office hours 9am-3pm, and on Saturday 8am-4pm.

1987 is Berlin's 750th anniversary and many celebrations will take place. The IBA (International Building Exhibition) has built 4000 buildings since 1978 leading up to this event. Although Berlin is essentially a 19th century city this programme should centre on the new Berlin of the 20th century.

Transport

Public transport in Berlin is first class; there's hardly a place which doesn't connect up with an 'U', 'S', or bus line. The underground ('U') is the fastest method and trains are very freqeuent. All forms of transport are punctual and there's rarely a hold-up. For all transport information contact the BVG (Berliner Verkehrs Betrieb) Potsdamer Straße 188, 1000 Berlin 30, Telephone 2165088 day and night. The BVG Linienienetz (map and guide) also gives all information and includes a full list of connections to all the main theatres, museums, concert-halls, cultural centres, parks, and other places of interest.

U Bahn The blue 'U' sign marks out all the underground stations. Trains run from 4am until between midnight and 1am and on Saturday until between 1 and 2am. The network map is easy to follow and most of Berlin can be reached by underground.

S Bahn Overground trains. Some of the S-Bahn stations (noted by their green and white sign) are worth visiting as monuments to a past age and for their early twentieth century architecture. Though not as many connections nor as frequent as the underground a lovely way to travel.

Bus Most day buses run every 10 minutes or so; every 20 minutes or so for most night connections. Drivers call out stops and names of streets which is a help and they will give you a personal reminder at a stop if asked. There are also special excursions buses to places like the Pfaueninsel or to Wansee beach. Tickets are bought from the driver unelss you already have a Sammelkarte etc.

Fares Within the time limit of 90 minutes, and as long as you travel in one direction, you can change as many times as you like, all on one ticket for 2.10DM. This ticket can be used on all forms of public transport. There are cheaper means of transport such as the Sammelkarte, a number of tickets at a cheaper rate on one card, and there are weekly tickets, monthly tickets, group and tourist tickets, and so on. There are no barrier checks on the trains but spot checks are made and the guilty fined.

Taxis Taxis are usually parked in queues at stands and one can hail them whil they are driving. Fares are reasonable.
For information about trains to and from West Germany see the Bundesbahnauskunft at the Pavillion am Zoo, Hardenbergstraße 20, 1000 Berlin 12, Telephone 312.1042. Open Monday-Friday 8.30am-6.30pm, Saturday 8.30am-1pm.
All flight information — telephone 4101-2306.

Sea Cafe with artificial island built by Engelbert Kremser

Sightseeing Tours

Severin & Kühn-Berliner Stadtrundfahrt: Leaves from Kurfürsten-damm 216. Telephone 883.1015.

Berolina Sightseeing Tours: Leaves from corner Kurfürstendamm and Meinekestraße. Telephone 8833131.

Berliner Bären-Stadtrundfahrt Leaves from corner Kurfürsten-damm and Rankestraße. Telephone 8836002.

BVB Stadtrundfahrten, Leaves from Kurfürstendamm corner Joachimstalerstraße. Telephone 8822063.
For information about group tours ask at the Berlin Information centre.

Banks: Generally open weekdays from 9am-1pm and on two after-noons, but each bank is different here. Some large stores also have brances which are open the same hours as their shopping hours.

Money Exchange Places/Wechselstube: are open longer than banks, for instance in Bahnhof Zoo or the Europa Center.

Post Offices: are open on weekdays from 8am-6pm and on Satur-day mornings 8am to 12 noon. NOTE:The Post Office at the Bahnhof Zoo is always open. The Tegel Airport Post Office is open daily from 6.30am-10.30pm.

POSTE RESTANTE

Mail can be sent to Bahnhof Zoo, D-1000 Berlin 12; enquiries: Telephone 313.9799.

Normal Shopping Hours

are Monday-Friday 9am-6pm. Some main shopping areas like the city centre and larger suburbs stay open until 6.30pm. Saturday shopping is from 9am-1/2 pm (depending on the shop and the area) and the **first** Saturday of each month, as well as the last four Saturdays before Christmas, are full shopping days from 9am-6pm.

EMERGENCY TELEPHONE NUMBERS

POLIZEI / Police: 110
Police—Lost Property: 699-1
FEUERWEHR / Fire & Ambulance: 112
NOTARZT / Emergency Doctor: 310031
ZAHNARZT / Emergency Dentist: 114
TIERARTZ / Emergency Vet: 772.1064
APOTHEKEN / Emergency Chemist: 114
TELEFON SEELSORGE (Counselling, like the Samaritans) 11101.

Trees

In the summer West Berlin is itself virtually one large park for there is hardly a street not lined with trees. Added to this 'torte' is whipped cream; the city has more than 60 parks, in addition to the Botanical Gardens and the forests such as the Grunewald and the Spandauer, Tegler or Düppler forests. Palaces such as Charlottenburg and Glienicke are also surrounded by exquisite gardents. In addition, listed below, are some other parks to enjoy:

Der Insulaner, in South Schöneberg
Stadpark Steglitz
Tiergarten, in the inner city, Berlin's most well-known park, enormous and luscious.
Volkspark Rehberge, in Wedding.
Pfaueninsel, the beautiful Peacock Island, transport by ferry; see

Market day at the Winterfeldt Platz

also castles and gardens.
Lietzensee, a lake and park in Charlottenburg.
Koenerpark, in Neukölln.

Flea-Markets

Considerable range offered from junk to expensive antiques. A complete list of addresses is impossible as they are always springing up in new places. The expensive antique shop area is around Kurfürstendamm and its side streets, for instance Fasanenstraße, Schlüterstraße or Bleibtreustraße. The best junk shops are to be found in Kreuzberg, Schöneberg or Charlottenburg. For sheer number and variety of stands (and people) it would be hard to beat the flea market at Straße des 17 Juni, held on Saturdays and Sundays from 8am until about 3.30.

Berlin Night Life

Still famous, as it always was, for an outrageous number of Kneipe (pubs but different from the English variety), discotheques and nightclubs. Kneipe are a matter of taste and geography, it's just best to try them out, and you won't have to walk far to find one. Don't worry about closing times — there is no official closing time in West Berlin and this means that places say open until 3 or 4 and later.

Two very well-known and fashionable discotheques are **Jungle** in Nürnburger Straße which is trendy and fashion-conscious, and **Reimers** in York Straße, Kreuzberg, popular with the arty crowd.

As for night clubs — the four places of current interest are:

Cri du Chat in Joachimstaler Straße; underground, punk.

DNC in Damaschke Straße; trendy, fashionable.

First, in Joachimstaler Straße; what could be termed a more 'upper class' night-club.

La Vie en Rose, in the Europa Center; presents a programme, sometimes a transvestites show, frequented, among others, by the 'media crowd'.

RESTAURANTS AND CAFES

Berlin is not a place to diet. For a start, the bread! People cannot, they say, live by bread alone but Berlin would be a good place to try if one had to. There are, reputedly, 5000 different kinds of bread in Germany and from the variety available it seems as if they're all to be had in West Berlin. And then there's the mouthwatering array of different salamis, sausages, cold meats, herrings, meats, cheeses — and for those with a sweet tooth the unbelievable cakes, biscuits and tortes which are, incidentally, works of art to the eye as well as to the palate.

Each district has at least one market, usually held in the mornings from about 9-1 twice a week, selling meat, fish, dairy products, fruit, vegetables, household items, clothing, plants and, not to forget, bread. They're fun and the variety and quality of produce is high though not always cheaper than the supermarkets (also good). Not so cheap but *superb* is the **Ka De We** food section, offering the best of German and international food, giving you an insight into just what you and your money can feed on while in West Berlin.

Or if you are more inclined towards healthy living then each district also has a branch of Reformhaus — a health food chain, as well as at least one other health food shop with good stocks of grain, beans, bread, juices, unsprayed fruit and vegetables and so on. Natural cosmetics are also usually available in Reformhaus and health food shops.

You may, however, be fed up with do-it-yourself, lucky enough to be on holiday or even restricted with time because you are passing through here on business. Whatever, and wherever you happen to be in Berlin, you will never have to walk far to find a restaurant, an Imbiss or a pub. West Berlin offers a United Nations variety of restaurants to choose from, the service is generally expert and fast and restaurants are on the whole fairly casual — places to sit, talk, eat, read, relax, meet people, rather than places to 'get dressed up for on Saturday night'. (This may be because every night is Saturday night in West Berlin). There are of course also the intimate, candle-lit, restaurants as well. There is, you see, every kind of eating place available and they are usually open until well past midnight. YOU WILL NOT GO HUNGRY IN WEST BERLIN!

Alter Krug, Potsdamer Straße 3, 1000 Berlin 37, Telephone 801.5380.
You can smell the quality from outside... the best of Austrian cuisine and wines. The walls are lined with theatre posters; no wonder, the owner-chef was a member of the Austrian Ballet at the Wiener Volksoper. A place for all ages; prices are middle-range. Open Sunday-Friday 11.30-midnight, Saturday 6pm-midnight. Note July and August: open daily 6pm, Sunday from 11.30am.

al Castello, Spandauer Damm 23, 19, Telephone 321.5392.
Italian restaurant, friendly service, conveniently opposite Scholß Charlottenburg. Open daily 11am-1am

Pizzeria Amico, Knesebeckstraße 18, 1000 Berlin 12, Telephone 312.9381.
Yummy Italian food, famous for the enormus salads and as a student restaurant, situated as it is in the heart of bookshop Berlin. Open daily 11am-1am.

ashoka Taj, Leibnitzstraße 62, 1000 Berlin 12, Telephone 323.6074.
As good as eating Indian in London, but with that special Berlin atmostphere. Middle price range. Open Monday-Friday 5pm-midnight and weekends from midday on.

Cafe Einstein Kurfürstenstraße 58, 1000 Berlin 30, Telephone 261.5096.
Cafe and restaurant a little more expensive than some but compensated for by the surroundings, the people, (invariably full to

Cafe Einstein, Kurfurstenstrasse in Berlin Tiergarten

bursting point, being the unique, marvellous place it is).. ah that melting apple strudel. Programmes of music, performance, readings, cabaret in addition. Open daily 10am-2am.

Cafe Savigny, Grolmanstraße 53, 1000 Berlin 12, Telephone 312.8195.
Casual trendy cafe. Open weekdays 10am on, weekends 11am on. No closign time.

Cafe Merlin, Carmerstraße 17, 1000 Berlin 12, Telephone 312.8157.
Excellent food in the French style, opens early evening and stays open until breakfast, 9am or thereabouts!

Ciao Ciao, Kurfürstendamm 156, 1000 Berlin 31, Telephone 892.3612.
Just by Schaubühne an unofficial restaurant for the theatre-art crowd. Delicious Italian food. (just as well it is unofficial because it may remain a little more exclusive). Open daily 12pm-12am.

Diener, Grolmanstraße 47, 1000 Berlin 12, Telephone 881.5329.
Gets going after 10pm — only one problem then, it's difficult to find a seat. Traditional central European cafe style snacks or meals and an enticingly gossipy atmosphere.

Die Lampe, Behaimstraße 21, 1000 Berlin 10, Telephone 342.6145
Tasty and original alternative and normal food, no meat or fish. Not expensive, 20 minutes or so, walking from Schloß Charlottenburg. Open every day from 9 to midnight.

Die Zauberflöte, Bismarckstraße 90, 1000 Berlin 12, Telephone 313.8315.
First class restaurant serving an international menu. Try the pepper steak or fresh salmon and all for middle price range. Opposite

the Deutsche Oper. Open every day from 6pm.

Ristorante Don Camillo, Schloßstraße 7-8, corner Neue Christstraße, 1000 Berlin 19, Telephone 322.3572.
Now this is really outstanding, not a place to stop off but a place to sit and talk and eat the best of Italian cuisine. And you have to admit, the service is perfect. Unbelievably all for middle price range. Only a few minutes from Scholß Charlottenberg so ideal for lunch or later; the opening times are 12-3pm and 6-11.30pm everyday except Wednesday.

Don Giovanni, Bismarckstraße 28, 1000 Berlin 10, Telephone 341.7653.
A smart Italian restaurant, a little more expensive than average but worth it. Old world atmosphere; the walls are graced with Italian antiques (genuine). Good combination with an evening at the opera a stone's throw away. Open Monday-Saturday from 5pm. Closed Sundays and holidays.

Exil, Paul-Lincke-Ufer 44a, 1000 Berlin 36, Telephone 612.7037.
An 'in' Kreuzberg restaurant, art crowd, excellent German food.

Florian, Grolmannstraße 52, 1000 Berlin 19, Telephone 313.9184.
Fashionable and COOL. Specialises in Southern German food... presented beautifully. Open daily 6pm-3am.

Fofi Estiatorio, Fasanenstraße 70, 1000 Berlin 15, Telephone 881.8785.
Like the Paris Bar or Exil one of *the* places for artists who have made it. It's worth being seen here and to be on kissing terms with those in the same league. But that's not all; the food — Greek — is truly first class, the service friendly and on the ball and the surroundings are a non-pretentious expampe of modern under-stated elegance. Open Monday-Saturday from 11.30am until 1am, or longer, and on Sundays from 7pm until... And during Berlin's beautiful, albeit too short, summer you can of course sit outside.

Galerie Terzo, Grolmanstraße 27/28, 1000 Berlin 12, Telephone 881.5261
Claimed by the owner to be the oldest student restaurant/cafe in West Berlin. Still student style; good late night atmosphere. Open Tuesday-Sunday 2pm-midnight.

Goya, Bismarckstraße 28, 1000 Berlin 12, Telephone 342.9102.
A Spanish restaurant, casual and informal, well cooked food (fish soup highly recommended) for middle price range. Close to the Deutsche Oper and it also has its own live music from 10pm each Friday and Saturday. Open Monday-Saturday 6-1.30am and on Sunday 4pm-midnight.

Holland Stüb'l Martin-Luther-Straße 11, 1000 Berlin 30, 1000 Berlin 248593.
Mainly Dutch and Indonesian cuisine, some international dishes. Open 5pm-1am; Sundays and holidays from midday-midnight.

Hotel Kempinski, Kurfürstendamm 27, 1000 Berlin 15, Telephone 88.10.91.
Berlin's most renowned hotel, in 1984 voted by the London Financial Times as one of the world's top ten. Also the home of Herbert von Karajan when he is in Berlin. The cafe, restaurant and grill are open to everyone — a combination of luxury, expertise and top quality cuisine. Kempinski Corner as it is fondly known in Berlin (the hotel is situated on the corner of the Kurfürstendamm and Fasanenstraße) is one of *the* places to sit and watch Berlin's main street.

King's Teagarden, Kurfürstendamm 217, 1000 Berlin 15, Telephone 883.7059.
The coffee is so good in Berlin that it's really not worth bothering about tea — except at this very fine tea place where one can chose from the 170 varieties or have one's own choice blended. (speciality of the house is the Alexander blend, worth trying). Subdued tasteful surroundings, international papers available. Open weekends 9-7pm, Saturday 9-2pm. Closed Sunday.

Kopenhagen, Kurfürstendamm 203-205, Telephone 881.6291/883.2503.
A fine Danish restaurant, traditional in style. Good for snacks after the theatre. Open from midday-midnight.

la Maddalena, Hagenstrasse 79, 1000 Berlin 33, Telephone 825.6580.
A marvellous Italian menu, comfortable setting and friendly service. Open 12pm-12am everyday.

Lavandevil, Schustehrusstraße 3, 1000 Berlin 10, Telephone 342.9280.
A typical Berlin combination of restaurnt-pub, but for its type hard to find in this part of Charlottenburg. Open Monday-Thursday and Sunday from 5pm-1am and on Friday and Saturday from 5pm-3am.

Latino, UhlandstraBe, 4/5, 1000 Berlin 12, Telephone 312.4046.
Lively, and invariably full Italian restaurant, close to the Hochschule der Künste, the DAAD as well as many galleries. Open everyday from 11am-1am.

Lebensbaum, Plalzburger Straße 20, 1000 Berlin 31, Telephone 875730.
For the biologically motivated... Vegetarian — no white sugar, no preservatives or other chemical additives. A *genuine* health food restaurant serving delicious, imaginative and cheap food! Should convert even the most ardent sceptics. Note also that galleries Milan, Fortsch and Andre are in the same street. Open Tuesday-Sunday from midday-midnight. Closed Monday.

Lotus House, Bismarckstraße 24, 1000 Berlin 12, Telephone 342.2392.
Tasty Chinese food in an informal, friendly atmosphere. Close to the Deutsche Oper. Closed Monday, otherwise open from midday-11.30pm.

Max und Moritz, Oranienstraße 162, 1000 Berlin 61, Telephone 614.1045.
Quite famous in Berlin — serves German food and specialises in yummy 'old Berlin' (Alt Berliner) dishes. Open everyday from 6pm onwards. Note, a theatre above, not part of restaurant but a joint visit could be combined.

Restaurant Luise, Königen-Luise-Straße 40, 1000 Berlin 33, Telephone 832.8487.
A few minutes from the Dahlem Museums, a relaxed and open atmosphere, especially lovely to sit under the trees in the summer. To make up for the winter the menu is bigger! Specialises in German food, for example liver with apple and onions, or sumptuous herring dishes. And delightful breakfasts are served until 3pm. Not expensive. Open each day from 10am-1am.

Paris Bar, Kant Straße 152, 1000 Berlin 12, Telephone 313.8052.
This is THE meeting place for the art-made-it-crowd in Berlin, and generally the art café. The menu, a la carte, changes daily — and is the best of French cuisine. Middle price range. Open everyday except Sunday from 12pm-1am or so.

Pasta Basta, Knesebeckstraße 94, 1000 Berlin 12, Telephone 3112.5982.
Another Knesebeckstraße favourite. 70 varieties of pasta are offered — definitely of mouth-watering standard. Open from 11am-1am.

Piazza, Savignyplatz 13, 1000 Berlin 12, Telephone 312.3990.
Mixture of Greek and Italian food — can't really lose! Open everyday from 11am-1am.

Pierre, Schaperstraße 17, 1000 Berlin 15, Telephone 881.1214.
Informal French restaurant opposite Freie Volksbühne. Open from Monday-Friday midday-2am; Saturday and Sunday and holidays 6pm-2am.

Pizzeria Venezia, Königen-luise-Straße corner Brümmerstraße, 1000 Berlin, Telephone 832.4647.
This Pizzeria is housed in an 80 year old building which has always been a restaurant. It doesn't look flashy but the food is great. A favourite with students — the 'Studenten-Pizza' and 'Studenten-Spaghetti' cost only 4DM or thereabouts. Open everyday from 11am-1am.

Preußen Hof, Spandauer Damm 3-5, Telephone 341.1020.
Cafe and restaurant opposite Scholß Charlottenburg, nostalgically styled in 'old Berlin' atmosphere. Traditional German food. Café breakfast from 7,30am, restaurant opens daily at midday.

Restaurant Maitre, Podbielskiallee 31, 1000 Berlin 33, Telephone 832.6003.
Restaurant Maitre is known as Berlin's top restaurant. It is one of the best French restaurants in Europe (which means the world) and it has been written up as *the* best French restaurant in Europe which is quite something when one thinks of Paris! Need one say

Cafe Mora, an artist and writer's cafe in Kreuzberg

more? Only, perhaps, that it offers a modern French cuisine based on classical French cooking where the natural tastes of different foods are preserved. Most of the products are brought in especially from France. Open Monday-Saturday from 7pm.

Rosati, Bismarckstraße 88, 1000 Berlin 12, Telephone 312.8368.
Quiet, intimate very fine Italian restaurant by the Deutsche Oper. Quality affirmed by its loyal clientele. Fish dishes especially recommended. Prices middle-range upwards. Open daily from midday-1am.

Ristorante Puccini, Bismarckstraße 99, 1000 Berlin 12, Telephone 312.2814.
Also by the Oper, the restaurant with an original taste and flair successfully combining traditional and nouvelle cuisine, Italian and international dishes. Always full and busy, frequented loyally by singers from the Oper; their photos decorate the walls. Middle price range and first class service. Open from 11.30am-12.30am.

Roasalinde, Knesebeckstraße 16, 1000 Berlin 12, Telephone 313.5996.
Fashionable cafe to sit and talk, light casual meals. Open 9.30am-3am everyday.

Restaurant Hellenikon, Grolmannstraße 39, 1000 Berlin 12, Telephone 882.2995.
Delicious Greek restaurant, open from 4pm daily.

Spree-Athen, Leibnitzstraße 60, 1000 Berlin 12, Telephone 324.1733.
A taste of turn of the century Berlin. A large restaurant seating

120 people, offering typical Berlin specialities from a self service buffet. Open from 6pm-2am.

Sokrates, Joachimstaler Straße 21, 1000 Berlin 15, Telephone 881.6659.
First class food and genuine atmosphere, all Greek. Open from 12am-2am.

Sapporo Kan, Schlüterstraße 52, 1000 Berlin 12, Telephone 881.2973.
If you are in the mood for a contrast to the heavier central European cuisine this is a very fine restaurant offering a full variety of delicate Japanese dishes. Open from 6pm to midnight everyday.

Sale & Pepe, Dahlmannstraße 19, 1000 Berlin, Telephone 323.2791.
Sicilian food served with imagination and of high quality. A lively, casual atmosphere, middle price range. Open from 6pm-4am each day.

Tessiner-Stuben, Bleibtreustraße 33, 1000 Berlin 15, Telephone 881.3611.
A brief look in the visitor's book will show the array of stars frequenting this exquisite restaurant: Herbert von Karajan, Rudolf Nureyev, Claudio Abbado, Micahel Caine, Jacqueline Bisset, Itzach Oistrakh, Leslie Caron. . . but you too can go there. The food is an original mixture of Swiss and French nouvelle cuisine and house secrets. Upper price range. Open daily from 6pm-1.30am; from Monday-Friday for lunch as well as midday-3pm.

Theater Restaurant, Uhlandstraße 28, 1000 Berlin 15, Telephone 881.4268.
A theatre restaurant since 1948, so-called because it is situated behind Kommödie and Theater am Kurfürstendamm. Serves a variety of German and international specialities cooked with homely flavour and care. Try the Berlin speciality of liver topped with apple and onions. Open daily from 11.30. Not expensive.

Toulouse, Lietzenburger Straße 86, 1000 Berlin , Telephone 883.4494.
Outstanding French rustic food. And wonderful freshly squeezed orange juice on tap. Open daily from 6pm-1am.

Waldhaus, Onkel-Tom-Straße 50, 1000 Berlin 37, Telephone 813.7575.
A traditional German beer garden, delightful barbecues in the summer. Menu mainly German and some French dishes. An international variety of breakfasts are offered, ranging in price from 5DM to the champagne breakfast for 101DM. Watch out though, no credit cards accepted! Open weekdays 5pm-1am and Saturday and Sunday 10am-1am.

Zille Stuben, Richard-Wagner-Straße 13, 1000 Berlin 10, Telephone 342.1414. From the outside one would expect to walk into a traditional Kneipe; with surprise you open the door to a turn of the century sitting room, the walls lined with Zille reproductions. The chef serves food successfully achieving the aim of tasting like 'mother's cooking' (try the Bratkatoffeln), and the atmosphere is *en famille*. You can also just sit and enjoy a drink or two. Close to the Oper. Closed Saturdays, open every other day from 6pm.

EAST BERLIN

For visitors to Berlin at least a day visit to East Berlin is essential, to have a broad view of the city of Berlin as it once was and as it is now, a divided city. Foreigners need to take a passport and buy a day visa (Tagesvisum) which is available at border points, Friedrichstrasse Station and Checkpoint Charlie for car travellers and pedestrians. A day visa lasts until midnight. You must exit at the same point that you entered East Berlin. Remember to allow for possible queues. The visa costs 5 Marks and a minimum amount of 25 Marks must be exchanged to East Berlin marks. Obviously more can be taken over to spend on East German products.

Many museums and centres are within walking distance from each other, so with advance planning and checks on opening times, much ground can be covered in a day. East Berliners are very happy to help if you lose your way. Restaurants accept foreign currency in case your East German marks run out.

Books, records, sheet music and exhibition catalogues are good buys in East Berlin. You may have to queue to enter a bookshop or restaurant. You must not take in books, newspapers, magazines, tapes but you can take in cameras and film and travel materials. When you leave it is forbidden to take out most foodstuffs, clothing and East German marks. If photographing and you have no desire to have an involuntary stay in East Berlin then avoid shots of the wall, border facilities, military installations, industrial and railway complexes. Illegal money exchange

View across the Wall Berlin Duppel

is also best avoided and if driving don't even take one glass of beer as alcohol is forbidden for drivers and penalties can be harsh.

Tickets can be booked for concerts and theatres on arrival in East Berlin. A list follows of museums, concert halls, theatres and bookshops to visit. Much of East Berlin is the old part of the city so there are interesting buildings to see as well as modern East Berlin at Alexanderplatz and Fernsehtrum. Other points of interest are Unter den Linden, the famous pre war Berlin boulevard, and Karl Marx Allee the new one.The Pergamon Museum has an exceptional collection as has the Nationalgalerie for paintings.

Berlin information
Information centre at the Television Tower Alexanderplatz 1020, Berlin. Tel: 2124675. Open Mon 1-7 Tues-Sat 9-7 and Sun 10-6.

For Foreigners (Tickets can be bought here)
Reiseburo Hochhaus Alexanderplatz 5 1020 Berlin. Tel 2154402 Mon-Fri 8-8 Sat and Sun 9-6

Wohin in Berlin?30 Pfennig at newsstands list East Berlin cultural events. West Berlin publications Tip and Zitty also list East Berlin theatres.

MAJOR MUSEUMS IN EAST BERLIN

Note opening times may change. Check in the latest 'Tip' or 'Zitty' magazine, or telephone direct from West Berlin.The connection is 0372.

Bodemuseum
Entrance Monbijoubrucke.
Open Wednesday-Sunday from 9am to 6pm. Friday 10am to 6pm. Includes Egyptian collection; Pre-Christian Byzantine collection; Sculpture Collection; Coin Collection and the Museum for early and Proto History; Children's Museum.

Fischergraben at the River-Spree, East Berlin

Pergamonmuseum
Entrance Kupfergraben, 1020 Berlin. Bodestrasse 1 - 3. Tel: 220 03 81.
Open daily, 9am - 6pm. Note that on Monday and Tuesday certain sections of the museum may be closed.
Sections include: Antiquities collection; Museum of the Near East; Islamic Museum, East Asian Collection, Museum of Ethnography.

Nationalgalerie
Entrance Bodestrasse
Open Wednesday - Sunday 9am - 6pm; Friday 10am - 6pm
Sections include galleries of 19th and 20th century painting.

Altes Museum
Entrance Lustgarten.
Open Wednesday - Sunday 9am - 6pm; Friday 10am - 6pm.
20th Century painting; the Nationalgalerie Archives; Prints and Drawings Collection.

Museum of Arts and Crafts/Applied Arts
1170 Berlin,Schlofs Kopenick
Wednesday - Saturday 9am - 5pm, Sunday 10am - 6pm.

Otto Nagel — Havs
1020 Berlin, Am Markischen Ufer 16/18, Tel: 279 1973/74
Open Sunday, Monday, Tuesday and Thursday, 10am - 6pm, Wednesday 10am - 8pm
Works by Otto Nagel; other works emphasising proletarian-revolutionary and anti-facist themes.

Museum of German History
1086 Berlin, Unter den Linden 2, Tel: 200 0591
Open Monday - Thursday 9am - 6pm (admission until 5pm)
Saturday and Sunday 9am - 4pm (admission until 3pm)

Gedenkstatte Berlin — Karlshorst/Memorial-place Berlin-Karlshorst
1157 Berlin-Karlshorst, Fritz-Schmenkel-Strasse, Tel: 508 4839
Open Tuesday - Friday 9am - 1pm and 3pm - 6pm.
Saturday 9am - 2pm and Sunday 9am - 4pm; closed last Saturday of each month.
Memorial museum in honour of the Soviet Union's victory over Germany in World War Two.

Markisches Museum
1020 Berlin, Am Kollnischen Park 5, Tel: 279 3728/29
Open Wednesday — Saturday 9am - 5pm, Sunday 9am - 6pm.
A museum devoted to the history and culture of Berlin

Natural Science Museum
1040 Berlin, Invalidenstrasse 43; Tel: 28970
Open Tuesday - Sunday 9.30am - 5pm.

Postal Services Museum of the DDR
1066 Berlin, Leipziger Strasse corner Mavestrasse; Tel: 231 2202

Johannes R. Becher Haus The house of the poet Becher and a literary museum.
1110 Berlin-Miederschonhausen, Majakowskinng 34; Tel: 482 6162
Open Tuesday 2pm - 6pm, Wednesday and Thurday 9am - 12pm and 2pm - 5pm, Friday 9am - 12pm, Saturday 9am - 12pm by appointment only.

Brecht-Haus Berlin
1040 Berlin, Chausseestrasse 125
Tel: 282 6067 Brecht Centre
282 7441 Brecht Archive
Open Monday - Friday 8am - 5pm
Study and living rooms of Brecht open Tuesday-Friday 10am -12pm, Thursday 5-7pm, Saturday 9.30am-12pm and 12.30-2pm (half hourly guided tours)
Archive is open by appointment only.

Hugenottenmuseum
1080 Berlin, Platz der Akademie, Franzosisches Kirche
Tel: 229 1760
Open Monday-Friday 10am-5pm
History of the French Reformation and the Hugenottes in Germany.

Robert Koch Museum
1080 Berlin, Clara-Zetlun Strasse 96
Tel: 220 2411
Open Monday-Friday 9am-1pm
Museum in honour of the founder of Microbiological Medicine, Robert Koch who in 1905 also received the Nobel Prize for his work on tuberculosis.

Ernst Busch Haus
1110 Berlin, Leonhard-Frank Strasse 11, Tel: 482 5702

East Berlin — Cathedral, TV tower, House of the Republic, Bridge built by Schinkel

Open Tuesday from 9am-1pm and Wednesday 2pm-7pm
(Group tours by appointment) Museum in honour of singer and ac-
tor Ernst Busch.

CLASSICAL
Main Concert Hall: Schauspielhaus, Platz der Akademie
Orchestras: Berliner Symphonie Orchester. Rundfunk Symphonie
Orchester. Staatskappelle. Orchester der Komische Oper
The Hochschule fur Musik Hanns Eisler in Otto-Grotenohl-Strasse
also holds concerts.
The main music shop for instruments: Rathaus Passagen, near
Alexanderplatz

THEATRES

Deutsche Staatsoper
Unter den Linden; Tel: 20540
(Traditional Opera)

Komische Oper
Behrenstrasse 55-57; Tel: 220 2761
(Realistic music theatre)

Metropol Theater
Friedrichstrasse 101/102; Tel: 200 0651

Deutsches Theater
Schumannstrasse 13a - 14: Tel: 28710
The renovated Max Reinhardt Theatre.

Kammerspiele
Schumannstrasse 13a - 14; Tel: 28710

Theater im Palart
Marx-Engels Platz, 1020 Berlin; Tel: 236 3345

Berliner Ensemble
am Bertolt Brecht-Platz; Tel: 288 80
(Mainly Brecht plays and in 'Brechtian' style-unique)

Maxim Gorki Theater
Unter den Linden; Tel: 207 1843/207 1790

Volksbuhne
Am Luxemburgplatz; Tel: 282 9607

Theater der Freundschaft
1156 Berlin, Hans-Rodenberg Platz 1; Tel: 55700
(for children and young people)

Das El in der Spielstatte
im Friedrichstadtpalast, Friedrichstrasse 107; Tel: 282 4690

Maxim Gorky Theater
Unter den Linden
(Mainly Russian/Soviet theatre)

Major Cultural Centres and Libraries

Akademie der Kunste
Hermann-Matem Strasse 58 - 60; Tel: 28780

Ausstellungzentrum am Fernsehturm
Karl-Liebknecht Strasse; Tel: 210 4296
Daily from 10am-7pm

Neuer Marstall
Am Marx-Angels Platz 7; Tel: 238 3287
Tuesday-Sunday 10am to 6pm

Berliner Stadtsbibliothek (Berlin State library)
Breite Strasse 32-34*
Monday 2-9pm, Tuesday-Friday 9am to 9pm, Saturday 9am-4pm

Deutsche Stadtsbibliothek
Unter den Linden 8; Tel: 20780
* Open 9am-9pm, Saturday 9am-5pm, Sunday closed.
Note! Also in Breite Strasse the Ratsbibliothek specialising in the history of Berlin.

Pionierpalast 'Ernst Thalmann'
An der Wuhlheide; Tel: 63527
Daily 10am-midnight

Palast der Republik
Marx-Engels-Platz; Tel: 238 2354/52
Daily 10am-midnight

Note: Galleries
For information about galleries see the latest 'Kunstblatt' magazine or 'Tip' or 'Zitty'.

Bookshops Specialising in the Arts

Bertolt Brecht Buchhandlung in Chaussee Strasse and the **International Buchhandlung** in Spandauer Strasse.
Both also sell records and the latter specialises in Russian literature and music.

Picture Theatres
The three main picture theatres are:
International in Karl-Marx-Allee
Kosmos in Krankfurter Allee
Colosseum in Schonhauser Allee
Note: also: **Film Theater Babylon** Rosa Luxembourg Platz and the **Film Library** in Kronen Strasse.

Irene Blumenfeld — the author

Irene Blumenfeld was born and brought up in New Zealand. She studied at Auckland University gaining a Bachelor of Arts degree in English Literature, History and Art and History, and a Master of Arts in English Literature. She worked as a magazine editor and bookseller before leaving New Zealand. She was a bookshop manager at the National Theatre in London before going to live in Berlin. Her parents were both born and brought up in Germany and her father's family came from Berlin. She is now a commissioning editor at Lund Humphries.

FIAC 86
25 OCTOBRE · 2 NOV.

PARIS · GRAND · PALAIS

TOUS LES JOURS DE 12 H À 19 H 30
SAMEDI, DIMANCHE 10 H À 19 H 30
NOCTURNE JEUDI 30 DE 12 H À 23 H.

DESSIN André Morain